Gay for Pay

The Blake & Clay Plays

Gay for Pay
The Blake & Clay Plays

Featuring:
Gay for Pay with Blake & Clay

Blake & Clay's Gay Agenda

Curtis Campbell & Daniel Krolik

Gay for Pay: The Blake & Clay Plays
first published 2024 by Scirocco Drama
An imprint of J. Gordon Shillingford Publishing Inc.
© 2024 Curtis Campbell & Daniel Krolik

Scirocco Drama Editor: Glenda MacFarlane
Cover design by Doowah Design
Author photo of Curtis Campbell by Kevin Connery
Author photo of Daniel Krolik by Denise Grant
Production photos by Kevin Connery

Printed and bound in Canada on 100% post-consumer recycled paper.

Production inquiries to:
gayforpayproductions@gmail.com

Library and Archives Canada Cataloguing in Publication

Title: Gay for pay : the Blake and Clay plays : featuring Gay for pay with Blake & Clay & Blake & Clay's gay agenda / Curtis Campbell & Daniel Krolik.
Names: Campbell, Curtis, 1994- author. | Krolik, Daniel, author. | Container of (work): Campbell, Curtis, 1994- Gay for pay with Blake & Clay. | Container of (work): Campbell, Curtis, 1994- Blake & Clay's gay agenda.
Identifiers: Canadiana 20240455215 | ISBN 9781990738609 (softcover)
Subjects: LCGFT: Drama.
Classification: LCC PS8605.A54295 G39 2024 | DDC C812/.6—dc23

We acknowledge the financial support of the Canada Council for the Arts, the Government of Canada, the Manitoba Arts Council, and the Manitoba Government for our publishing program.

J. Gordon Shillingford Publishing
P.O. Box 86, RPO Corydon Avenue, Winnipeg, MB Canada R3M 3S3

To our wives

Curtis Campbell

Curtis Campbell is a playwright, novelist, and director. His debut novel, *Dragging Mason County*, was released to critical acclaim in 2023. It was described by Daniel MacIvor as "the teenage love child of David Sedaris and John Waters." Curtis lives in Toronto with an artist named Kevin and their dog, Pip.

Daniel Krolik

Daniel Krolik is a performer and writer. His acting credits include work with Studio 180, Buddies in Bad Times, Roseneath Theatre, Magnus Theatre, Sudbury Theatre Centre, Bluewater Summer Playhouse, Repercussion Theatre, and the Next Stage Theatre Festival. Daniel was named an "Artist to Watch" by *NOW Magazine* and has co-written the plays *Point of Departure* and *Release the Stars: The Ballad of Randy & Evi Quaid*. Daniel also co-hosts the popular podcast *BGM: Bad Gay Movies/Bitchy Gay Men*.

Acknowledgements

Our thanks go first and foremost to Laura Anne Harris for her supreme generosity.

Thank you to Rachel Kennedy and James Hyett for saying yes, many times over.

Thank you to Kevin Connery at The Square Shop for his generosity, and for always making Blake & Clay look so good.

We extend our deep appreciation to the people who saw what we were doing and helped us do it. Glen Sumi, Rob Kempson, Freddy Frenette, Cam Johnston, Julian Buloff, Victor Pokinko, Marie Beath Badian, Alia Rasoul, David Mallette, Adam Bromley, Laura Paduch, Chris Abraham, Paolo Santalucia, Brian Francis, Zack Liebzeit, and the many Toronto Fringe goers who spread the word of Blake & Clay.

We gratefully acknowledge the generous support of Studio 180 and Tarragon Theatre, offered through the invaluable Ontario Arts Council Recommenders Grant program.

Our final thanks are to Jonathan Wilson, even if "thank you" doesn't quite cover it. He is the third creator of Blake & Clay. Both plays were formed in the crucible of the Toronto Fringe and guided by Jonathan's comedic savantry. His hands, and expert buffoonery, are all over these plays. Thank you, Jonathan. We are smudged with your fingerprints and have no intention of wiping them off.

Playwrights' Notes

In his review of *Gay for Pay with Blake & Clay*, Glenn Sumi wrote "There's plenty of anger simmering beneath the script's surface, especially in an audience participation section on fighting back. (You know you're at an exciting show when some audience members go *'Whoa!'*)"

I've been fixated on that *Whoa* since the night of that review. It was a sold-out performance, and our audience was rowdy enough to add just over five minutes to our usual runtime. This audience began their participation as soon as Blake & Clay bounded on stage. By the scene referenced in Sumi's review, the energy in the room was reaching a fever pitch. I believe it made that moment of *Whoa* even more shocking.

Shock value is often an empty gesture, as it tends to prioritize subject matter over delivery. But if our audience was shocked, then I do see that shock as having value. The scene referenced by Sumi is called *More Than A Victim: Adversity for the Unadversed*. Beneath an otherwise silly bit of audience participation is that simmering anger, which we invited our audience to share in. Blake & Clay begin *Gay for Pay* by casting their audience as straight men training to play gay roles. The irony is that the audience was usually full of gay men who inherently understood the joke being played out on stage.

Critique of queer representation tends to be pointed outward, at the gatekeepers and the hegemony and the corporate conglomerates. Much of both *Blake & Clay* scripts are pointed outward as well. But there is also an underlying critique pointed toward our community. A critique of the queer tendency towards infighting, moral panic, and reactionary puritanism.

A critique of the navel-gazing and self-aggrandizement so often present in queer art. But the critique underscoring both plays is an often scathing indictment of our own complicity. It's a complicity that isn't without reason. Our survival often hinges on perpetuating the heterocentric worldview. Gay men may not always have to pretend at heterosexuality, but we are required to edit and curate ourselves in order to survive a world built around it. However, Blake & Clay are both tired of surviving. They want to thrive. Which is why they try, in both plays, to wrap the queer experience with an inoffensive and user-friendly bow.

Queer people are cockroaches. We have thriving night lives, we are consummate survivors, and we are attracted to crumbs. *Gay for Pay* ends with Blake & Clay gleefully taking the crumbs offered by Hollywood. *Gay Agenda* sees Blake & Clay attempting to unite all queer people by writing a manifesto that is ultimately an offering of crumbs. Underpinning both plays is an obsession with queer representation in art and media, and a comedic plundering of the expectations placed on it. Queer discourse is often occupied by the topic of queer representation, and it is sometimes difficult to see this as anything but a preoccupation. It can feel as if there's a buck being passed, as if we're handing the reins of queer liberation to the gatekeepers and hegemony and corporate conglomerates. There is the distinct possibility that queer culture is outsourcing the queer revolution to organizations who will always try to sell it back to us at a profit. The line between queer representation and queer gentrification may be thinner than we'd like to believe. Which is why I believe that if the queer revolution is to be televised, our salvation will not be found on a streaming platform. Our salvation lies somewhere inside that *Whoa*. It lives in the shock of discovering your own anger. It lives in what you decide to do with it.

—*Curtis Campbell*

The two *Gay for Pay* plays have been both the most symbiotic collaboration I've had working with other artists, and the most rewarding experience I've ever had working in the theatre. When we started work on *Gay for Pay with Blake & Clay*, we were still deep in the throes of pandemic life. Theatre was just starting a bumpy road to coming back and new seasons were being announced, but the collateral damage after two years of solitude had left me bereft of any hope for a professional or artistic future. There wasn't anything for me to do but to pour out all my rage and loneliness into our script. No one was expecting anything, and we had absolutely nothing to lose.

So we wrote.

I didn't know we had something anyone would respond to until our tech run during Fringe at the Tarragon. Our two house techs were our entire audience. There is one moment towards the end of the play — when Blake says, "But if us queers have learned anything while living beneath a system of violence and oppression…" he can't finish the thought, and a long and uncomfortable silence follows. During that silence, our techs responded with a mixture of laughter and horror that was exactly what we were hoping to hear. After the preceding two years, it turned out to be a transformative moment. Blake is angry — at being ignored, at aging out of whatever the gay community finds desirable, at decades of being told by the non-gay powers that be what is and isn't "the right kind of gay." To hear that anger acknowledged in real time after those last couple of years was seismic.

By the time we were writing *Blake & Clay's Gay Agenda*, it dawned on me that I was a part of something incredibly unique — a coming-together of three separate generations of gay men, both onstage and off. This rarely happens in the theatre, let alone in gay life. The working relationship that developed between me, Curtis, and the demented genius Jonathan Wilson was so effortless and cut so deep. Our very different histories and perspectives — towards sex, politics, pop culture — gave our work a specificity and a depth I could have never found on my own. And the more we mined ourselves for material, the louder our audiences laughed.

At a moment in time when joy is in perilously short supply, bringing these two plays to life has filled me with unprecedented joy. Thank you for reading these and for meeting us at the intersection of humour and anger. Liza Minnelli on the Home Shopping Network said it best — "It was thrilling to talk to you, and I'll remember it."

—*Daniel Krolik*

Foreword

by Brian Francis

In 1982, a film called *Making Love* was released. Starring Kate Jackson, Michael Ontkean, and Harry Hamlin, the film was considered the first mainstream gay love story between two men. The actors, naturally, were straight. (You wouldn't be able to call it "mainstream" if they were queer.) I was eleven years old at the time and have a distinct memory of seeing the movie advertisement in my local newspaper. I knew the film was controversial, and although I was too young to really understand the significance, I knew that this movie was about me in some way.

It would be years before I saw a gay love story in movie theatres. That film was *Brokeback Mountain*. Again, starring straight actors playing gay. Afterwards, I kept thinking about how the film wouldn't have been nearly as commercially successful had a pair of openly gay actors taken on the lead roles. Why was that? Would a mainstream audience not consider *Brokeback Mountain* relevant to them? Was it that straight audiences (I'll go out on a limb here and say "straight female audiences") were titillated or intrigued by how convincing two straight male actors could portray same sex passion? Or was it simply that, when straight actors play gay, it feels safer to straight audiences? We know they're just actors, after all. Nothing on the screen was real. When cowboys Ennis and Jack kissed, it wasn't gay kissing. It was pretend. There was no threat. *Brokeback Mountain* was safe to watch because it was a movie about gay people made by — and made for — straight people.

When I first saw *Gay for Pay with Blake & Clay* at the Toronto Fringe Festival in 2022, I thought the play was many things. Hilarious, of course. Quick-witted, whip-smart, achingly astute. But more than anything, *Gay for Pay with Blake & Clay* felt like a whirlwind, as though a cork had been yanked from a bottle whose contents had been under pressure for years — years of denial and suppression. Self-doubt and ignorance. A demand for authenticity and representation in a world that didn't seem all that interested in what queer people felt, or thought, or said.

At some point in their formative years, most queer people understood that, to survive, they had to play a game. We had to pretend to be people we weren't to pass unnoticed and avoid detection. In short, we needed to be actors. Some of us weren't very good (yes, that was me at prom on the dance floor, lip-syncing to Madonna's "Vogue"), but most of us tried, as best as we could, to swallow ourselves up, rein it in, and dim our queer lights.

In *Gay for Pay with Blake & Clay* and *Blake & Clay's Gay Agenda*, there is much to laugh about. Krolik and Campbell's scripts read like arrows pointed at every angle imaginable, sharpened by their insightful observations. Yet, despite the laughter, there is anger that ripples below the surface. Humour and rage are never that far apart from one another. A prime example is Blake's uncomfortable confession to the "audience" of straight actors. "…I realized that the kind of gay I've been trying for isn't gay at all. It's you." The "you" he's addressing isn't just the audience; it's the straight world. Up until that point, we've enjoyed Blake and Clay tearing a new one into the hypocrisy, the stupidity, the absolute gall, of a society that holds back its queer people. But that turning point in the play is, without a doubt, its most truthful moment. It's the heart of the work, however broken and beaten that heart might be.

I realized, in writing this, that I'd never seen *Making Love*, so I sat down, all these years later, to judge it for myself. I was pleasantly surprised. It's well-acted, a bit melodramatic at times, but sincere in its intent. You can also find interviews with the actors on the internet, answering questions about why they took on the roles of two gay men when there would surely be fallout from Hollywood. Why take that kind of risk in terms of their careers? And while the actors' answers are thoughtful, and perhaps, a bit scripted, I couldn't help but think of the gay actors who never got to answer that question. They never had a shot. They were never even a consideration. Because to cast gay actors in those roles wouldn't have been safe. Imagine living in a world that constantly echoes the message that no one wants to hear your truth because no one thinks that truth has value.

There is nothing safe about Krolik and Campbell's work. It's biting, honest, devastating, and real. In other words, it's everything audiences need to hear. There's another bit of dialogue that resonates with me, spoken by Clay. "I always thought about the little gay boys at home who might be watching," he says. "And I hoped they were paying attention. It's easy to look down at it now. But I played those parts because the only way forward was through. And now it seems that we are through."

The irony, of course, is that we aren't through. We've made progress, sure. We have come a long way in terms of our visibility. We are testaments to authentic queer lives, regardless of society's definitions and boxes. We don't need to rely on movies made by straight people for representation. We have the internet. Apps. Even a Netflix category. We have one another. And we have Blake and Clay to tell us their truths. They've worked hard. Been in the business for years. They've seen it all.

The least we could do is listen.

Brian Francis is an award-winning writer whose works include Fruit, Natural Order, Break in Case of Emergency, Missed Connections: A Memoir in Letters Never Sent, a*nd the performance piece* Box 4901.

Production History

Gay for Pay with Blake & Clay premiered at the Tarragon Extra Space as part of the Toronto Fringe Festival on July 7, 2022, with the following company

Blake ....Daniel Krolik
Clay..Jonathan Wilson

Directed by Curtis Campbell
Stage Managed by James Hyett

Gay for Pay was the winner of the Second City Award for Outstanding Comedy, 2022, and was nominated for Outstanding New Play, Dora Mavor Moore Awards, 2023.

Blake & Clay's Gay Agenda premiered at the Tarragon Mainspace as part of the Toronto Fringe Festival on July 7, 2023, with the following company:

Blake ....Daniel Krolik
Clay..Jonathan Wilson

Directed by Curtis Campbell
Stage Managed by James Hyett
Produced by Rachel Kennedy

The production reopened at the Assembly Theatre as part of Bad Dog Theatre's Comedy on Queen Street on December 27, 2023.

Gay for Pay
with Blake & Clay

Characters

BLAKE and CLAY are middle-aged gay men. Clay is older than Blake.

Accompanying Blake & Clay is the pre-recorded voice of a NARRATOR. It should be voiced by a man and delivered with the cadence of the narrators from a 1950s instructional film, particularly the work of Coronet Films.

Setting

An acting class. The play is presented as a bare bones seminar and has no fourth wall. It should be explicitly set in whatever performance space or room it is literally in at the time. The audience is cast as straight male actors attending the seminar. Whether or not they are straight or male is immaterial, as the actors will treat them as such. The performers may deviate from the script to chat and improvise with the audience based on what is really happening in the room at the time. A common example of this during the original run was when Blake & Clay would welcome latecomers and catch them up on what they had missed.

Design

Two chairs in an otherwise bare space. Perhaps a projection screen. The original production of *Gay for Pay with Blake & Clay* made use of a projector and screen to provide scene titles, text, visual aids, and sight gags. They are entirely optional but are useful in keeping your audience on track and for delivering jokes. A few projections used in the original production have been noted and can be used or disregarded.

A Note on References

An asterisk* appears beside people, places, or things that are local to the original staging of this text. These references should be replaced with whatever your local or national equivalent is. Asterisks also appear over the names of celebrities and social media platforms which should be updated with the times as you see fit.

A Note on Music

The music used in the original production is noted throughout. Song choices are merely suggestions and can be used as written or disregarded.

Gay for Pay with Blake & Clay. Blake (Jonathan Wilson) and Clay (Daniel Krolik) playing Chasten and Pete in Love Chasten, A Gay Fantasia on National Themes. Photo by Kevin Connery, 2022.

Gay for Pay with Blake & Clay. Clay (Daniel Krolik) leads a pop quiz in More Than a Victim, Adversity for the Unadversed. Photo by Kevin Connery, 2022.

BLAKE & CLAY bound into the space to Lady Gaga's "Born This Way." They clap along with the audience, hamming it up. The song fades as:

BLAKE: I'm Blake!

CLAY: I'm Clay!

BLAKE: And you're—

BOTH: Straight!

BLAKE: And we all know why you're here.

CLAY: You need a little help to book the part that's going to take your acting career into the stratosphere!

BLAKE: And that's where our combined ninety-seven years of acting experience come in handy. Because we're not just actors. We're gay actors.

CLAY: We were a little nervous to lead a seminar exclusively for heterosexual men.

BLAKE: But then we reminded ourselves that the modern heterosexual is an enlightened breed.

CLAY: You truly are humanity's Goldendoodle.

BLAKE: Today's straight men are able to talk about their feelings!

CLAY: They moisturize their faces!

BLAKE: And one of these days you might even wash those darn buttholes!

CLAY: This new stock of heterosexual men *love* gay culture.

BLAKE: Take Harry Styles. He loves a dress, loves a pearl, and loves his series of hot, rich, celebrity girlfriends.

CLAY: You straights are putting in the work, and don't think we haven't noticed!

BLAKE: You're taking your girlfriends to the drag shows.

CLAY: You're getting drunk at the Pride parades!

BLAKE: And you're taking your girlfriends to the drag shows!

CLAY: But most importantly, you're playing us in film, television, and my first true love. The live theatre.

BLAKE: Because you're not just an audience full of heterosexual men, you're an audience full of heterosexual actors!

CLAY: You know, Blake, some of my favourite actors are straight men.

BLAKE: Yes! Tom Cruise.

CLAY: John Travolta.

BLAKE: Glenn Close.

CLAY: There is no greater challenge for a straight actor than to play gay.

BLAKE: But there is also no greater reward. Consider the Oscar wins of these straight men who bravely limped their wrists on screen:

CLAY: Mahershala Ali, *Green Book.*

BLAKE: Christopher Plummer, *Beginners.*

CLAY: Sean Penn, *Milk.*

BLAKE: Philip Seymour Hoffman, *Capote.*

CLAY: William Hurt, *Kiss of the Spider Woman.*

BLAKE: Tom Hanks, *Philadelphia.*[1]

CLAY: Brendan Fraser, *The Whale.* He played a morbidly obese, mentally ill gay man.

BLAKE: Which, in this business, is what we call a *triple threat.*

CLAY: Those gold statues were justly earned. Because it's not just a matter of throwing on a feather boa and some lesions.

BLAKE: It takes skill. Craft. Determination.

CLAY: And looking good in a knee-length silk kimono.

BLAKE: These actors earned Oscar gold while playing gay. And with the help of Blake and Clay, you can too.

CLAY: In this seven-part seminar we will teach you the cornerstones of acting, playing, and living gay.

BLAKE: When you walk out of here, you won't just be living your truth. You'll be living ours too.

Music plays as a NARRATOR announces the title of a new scene:

---

[1] Update the list of straight men who have won Oscars for playing gay roles at this point if needed.

LGBTQ+Y-O-U

CLAY: Queer life sure is full of terminology.

BLAKE: You're telling me that pansexuality has nothing to do with cooking?

CLAY: You're telling *me* that a throuple isn't some horrible, cystic skin growth?

BLAKE: Don't worry, 2SLGBTQIA+ isn't a streaming service.

CLAY: No spoilers! I still haven't seen WandaVision!

BLAKE: Kathryn Hahn once called me inappropriate on set!

CLAY: I'm terrified of Paul Bettany.

BLAKE: It's an all-inclusive acronym for anyone non-heteronormative. But today our audience is straighter than my posture when I played a gay army cadet who gets beaten to death with a pillowcase full of soap.

CLAY: Straighter than my first boyfriend.

BLAKE: Which means we need to spill the tea.

CLAY: Hold up, Blake. Spill the what?

BLAKE: The tea! For terminology!

BLAKE: Us gays live, laugh, and love to classify while we assify.

CLAY: Assify? Yassify!

BLAKE: But we're getting ahead of ourselves.

CLAY: Or behind!

BLAKE: Now watch it, Clay. That kind of talk is what got my lines cut from *A Bad Moms Christmas*!

CLAY:	Kristen Bell is my safe word!
BLAKE:	The ecology of the gay world is a zoological wonderland that would leave even Doctor Doolittle breathless.
CLAY:	Robert Downey Jr. hasn't been this breathless since he choked on his own vomit on the set of *Ally McBeal*.
BLAKE:	So join us, won't you? As we step into the lush wilderlands of The Gay Bestiary.
	Animal sounds and PBS documentary-style music plays.
CLAY:	These are the gay men that you'll find yourself embodying!
BLAKE:	I haven't embodied a gay man in months.
CLAY:	The Bear!
BLAKE:	Covered in hair?
CLAY:	You're a Bear.
BLAKE:	A chrome dome with a spare tire to match?
CLAY:	I do declare, you're a Bear!
BLAKE:	Chubby-cheeked upstairs and downstairs?
CLAY:	Call Smokey, bitch, cuz you're on fire.
BLAKE:	The Bear holds a place of reverence in the gay community.
CLAY:	They hold our history in their hairy fingers. Our stories in their leathery palms.
BLAKE:	As a Bear, you can expect to be playing gay bar bouncers.
CLAY:	Leather-clad motorcyclists.

BLAKE: Gruff construction workers who, plot twist, love Judy Garland!

CLAY: Sage elders with lessons to impart about life, love, and what happens when you neglect to use sunblock.

BLAKE: The Otter!

CLAY: What many consider to be the two-seater version of The Bear.

BLAKE: Smaller and tighter than their beary brethren, these svelte studs are hairy-chested and take pride in their appearance.

CLAY: They've opted for literal beards ever since ditching their college beards named Trisha or Jen.

BLAKE: Think The Otter might fit your frame? Expect to be cast as a brew-toting hipster gay.

CLAY: We're talking septum piercings and a love of the Berlin dungeon scene.

BLAKE: Remember, Otters tend towards the artistic. One in three self-identifies as a DJ.

CLAY: And unfortunately? One in two self-identifies as a spoken-word poet.

BLAKE: The Twink!

CLAY: The background player of the queer experience.

BLAKE: Twinks are young gays. Skinny and smooth.

CLAY: They're your Starbucks barista.

                              Projection: Bill Skarsgard as Pennywise the Clown

BLAKE: They're your sister's hairdresser.

Projection: Gollum

CLAY: They're every man to have ever majored in musical theatre.

Projection: A literal velociraptor

BLAKE: To play a Twink, simply study the facial movements of an alligator.

CLAY: When playing a Twink, remember: They do everything that a regular gay does, but backwards and in heels.

BLAKE: The Silver Fox!

CLAY: The leaner cousin to The Bear, The Silver Fox is a rarer breed to find in the wild.

BLAKE: Greying temples and pluming chest hair are the distinct markers of The Silver Fox. These middle-aged marvels age gracefully, embracing their markings as a display of beauty. Think George Clooney.* Pierce Brosnan.* Chris Meloni.*

> *BLAKE becomes lost in thought and begins to describe a sexual fantasy with Chris Meloni that becomes increasingly violent and graphic. CLAY gets him to snap out of it. This should be improvised with each performance.*

BLAKE: The Silver Foxes in the audience can expect to play guarded businessmen.

CLAY: Professionals who gave up on love when their long-term partner died of an unnamed illness.

BLAKE: A white-collared industrialist who makes sure that the children's home he grew up in gets everything it needs to stay open.

CLAY: The only thing he can't open?

BLAKE: Is his heart.

              They both sigh dreamily.

CLAY: The Gym Rat! These upside-down triangles are the factory setting for gays on screen.

BLAKE: The Gym Rat is the Insta-gay.

CLAY: The walking thirst trap.

BLAKE: The guy who always just got in from the airport.

CLAY: And he's not even jet-lagged.

              BLAKE searches the audience and identifies a Gym Rat.

BLAKE: We've got some Gym Rats in the audience today, Clay. What kind of roles do you think they can expect to play?

CLAY: Oh, great question. Hmmm. Gay firefighter?

BLAKE: Gay surgeon?

CLAY: Gay librarian.

BLAKE: Gay teacher.

CLAY: Gay garbage man.

BLAKE: Gay social worker.

CLAY: Gay accountant.

BLAKE: Gay parking attendant.

CLAY: Any gay part, really—

BLAKE: Just any breathing homosexual, if we're being honest—

CLAY: So! Whether you're a straight man who can play a gay Bear—

BLAKE: A straight man who can play a gay Otter—

CLAY: Or a straight man with enough abs to play the shy, self-effacing bookstore owner.

BLAKE: The roster of gay roles is your oyster!

CLAY: So grab a knife and get shucking!

BLAKE: We're passing the flaming baton to you!

CLAY: And remember to tell your casting director that you were trained at the hands of Blake & Clay.

The boys pause, waiting for the audience to respond.

They improvise with the audience. They ask about people's acting agents, about auditions, about networking opportunities. BLAKE & CLAY make it abundantly clear that they're ready and willing to take on any part until the NARRATOR announces the title of a new scene:

Standard Gay Moments

BLAKE: Playing a gay character will open you up to the infinite spectrum of the human experience.

CLAY: Which we've broken down for you. This is a sampling.

BLAKE: An amuse-bouche, if you will.

CLAY: Honey, my bouche hasn't been amused since
                    1982.

BLAKE: Gay characters sure have come a long way.
                    There is such a wide variety of situations
                    and moments and relationships and human
                    connections that we now get to play.

CLAY: Yes! And here are all sixteen of them.

                    *The NARRATOR reads the headings
                    while the boys step forward, one at a time,
                    and perform the corresponding snippet of
                    dialogue.*

NARRATOR: *Hairdresserly Admonishments*

BLAKE: I style hair, Claudia, I don't style doormats.
                    So how dare you let a man walk all over you
                    like that?

NARRATOR: *Defiantly Singing Show Tunes During an
                    Otherwise Sombre Moment*

CLAY: The police may have raided our bathhouses!
                    But they can never raid our spirit!

                    *CLAY begins to sing a rousing call-to-arms
                    song but is cut off by the next title.*

NARRATOR: *Speaking Wistfully About Your Dead Aunt.*

BLAKE: When Auntie Berdice found me in a pair of
                    Momma's white pumps, she gave me one
                    good look and said *now child, I know you're not
                    wearing white after Labour Day!* That's when
                    I knew that Auntie Berdice was the only
                    creature on God's green Earth who had ever
                    truly understood me.

NARRATOR: *Finally Telling Your Bigoted Brother-in-Law What's What*

CLAY: That's right. Clayton is my boyfriend, *and* my interior decorator.

NARRATOR: *Dying Bravely*

BLAKE: You're going to get that scholarship to Poetry College, and I'm going to beat Gay Cancer while looking *cough, cough* sickening.

NARRATOR: *Learning the True Meaning of Christmas*

CLAY: Wait, Max! Don't go. Christmas isn't just about the hot chocolate festival, or the gingerbread house competition, or even your niece's Christmas pageant. It's also about falling in love with the carpenter you always had a crush on in high school.

    CLAY mimes opening an engagement ring box.

    Merry Christmas, Max.

NARRATOR: *Rejecting Conversion Therapy*

BLAKE: I *am* your son, Dad! And the only converted thing in my life? Is the loft space that Trent and I just signed a lease on.

NARRATOR: *Over-Sharing with Your Drama Students*

CLAY: If you think I landed understudy to a Flying Monkey by "learning my lines" and "showing up on time" then you're in for more than just *egg* on your face, children.

NARRATOR: *Dispensing Sage Elderly Advice*

BLAKE: You can't give up now, Daxtonne! Not when your dance troupe has a shot at saving our town's only gay bar. My time on the dance floor is long behind me. After all, I'm thirty-seven.

NARRATOR: *Impassioned Plea to Local Representative*

CLAY: Those boys are someone's son, Councillor Chancellorson! But maybe you're too busy playing yacht-tennis on Vacation Island to see that.

NARRATOR: *Scathing Personal Assistant Standing in the Way of Heterosexual Love*

BLAKE: There is no way I'm letting you march that Old Navy–clad tuchus into Miss Delbatone's office. She's in the middle of a very important fashion merger! It's corseting season! Don't let the door hit your JC Penny on the way out.

NARRATOR: *Closeted Angry Pageant Father*

CLAY: Let me see teeth, Clarissa-Claire! Those Tijuanan surgeons didn't give you the most expensive smile on the menu for you to win *Miss Congeniality*!

NARRATOR: *If You Love Him, Go to Him*

BLAKE: The day that you left town was the best day of my life. Because I knew that, while I was losing a girlfriend, the world was gaining a girlboss. A girlboss with the toothy smile of one Julia Roberts, the Soul Cycled ass of one Jennifer Lopez, and the relentless drive to hunt down and kill terrorists as one Jessica Chastain in *Zero Dark Thirty*. A man?! You don't need no stinking man.

Now you get back out there. You find that man! And don't you dare come back without a wedding ring!

NARRATOR: *Midwestern Quarterback Comes Out to His Father*

BLAKE: Dad? I think I might enjoy the company of other men.

CLAY: Dad? I think I might be what they call a homosexual.

BLAKE: Dad? I think I might be a vers top with occasional bottom tendencies.

CLAY: Dad? I think I might try pumping my nipples for enhanced pleasure.

BLAKE: Dad? I think I might understand the unwritten rules of conduct for under-the-stall bathroom cruising in parks and public conservation areas.

NARRATOR: *Dangerous Stalker Who Thinks He Is a Hopeless Romantic*

BLAKE: She doesn't love you like I do, Bradley. Can't she see that? What we had in that darkroom can't just be some dark secret. So I'm doing this for your own good. Tell me you love me or I'll blind myself with these photo chemicals.

NARRATOR: *Horny Elderly Neighbour and His Cat*

CLAY gingerly picks up an imaginary cat.

CLAY: Now listen here, Priscilla. I don't want to see you go back to Angelo. Miss Betty Comden doesn't want to see you go back to Angelo. Do you, Miss Betty Comden? Do you? Although, if he ever decides to play for the right team, you tell him and his Italian sausage to pay us a house call!

An oven timer goes off.

Ooh! My Baked Alaska's ready.

The two shake off their work, making a meal out of their attempts to ground themselves back in the real world.

BLAKE: These are the hilarious and heartbreaking moments that you'll be hashtag blessed enough to play.

CLAY: Gay characters are a real character, am I right, Blake?

BLAKE: And as more queer writers get their time in the sun, these moments can only diversify! Because some might see these as a bit limited, right? I mean, it's not like this is the entire queer experience. That's kind of a—

They speak the following two lines simultaneously as CLAY rushes to get in the way of BLAKE's sudden need to speak candidly.

CLAY: Which is to say that, if ever in doubt, you need simply return to your Standard Gay Moments by Blake and Clay. These will be your tent-poles, your compass as you act your way through the many letters of the LGBTQ+ spectrum! Remember!

BLAKE: That's the thing about this business. You start off with all these possibilities, and they start getting sanded down, and shrunk, and after a while you're left feeling grateful for any bit of work you can get.

BLAKE speaks continually, but he stops and goes completely silent when CLAY says the word "Remember!" BLAKE should improvise text if he needs to fill time before that.

CLAY: It's not basic. It's foundational!

Music plays as a NARRATOR announces the title of a new scene:

Gay Sex: A Beginners Guide

CLAY: Something that a lot of straight actors worry about is being called upon to perform a sex scene. A *gay* sex scene. But these are the same worries that Blake and I experience while *having* gay sex.

BLAKE: What do I do? Does my body look good enough? Where does everything *go*? Will my mom see this?

CLAY: Let's have a frank intercourse about gay sex.

BLAKE: Gay sex is a lot like your fantasy football league. You trade stats for a while before everyone leaves disappointed.

CLAY: Gay sex is a lot like a Super Bowl party. Sometimes there are lots of guys, but sometimes it's just you and a work friend with marital troubles.

BLAKE: Gay sex is a lot like a Marvel movie. Lots of middle-aged white guys who have to hire a personal trainer and a nutritionist before they show up.

CLAY: Gay sex is a lot like a game of paintball. You try to come out on top, but mostly you're just tired and covered in goo.

BLAKE:	With a fair amount of bruising.
CLAY:	You know Blake, I've spent a fair amount of time on film sets.
BLAKE:	It's true. Clay was an extra in *The Incredible Hulk*.[2]
CLAY:	Edward Norton threw coffee at my shins when he heard he wasn't getting the final cut of the film.
BLAKE:	What a thrill.
CLAY:	It was an honour to witness his process.
BLAKE:	Have you ever filmed a gay sex scene, Clay?
CLAY:	Not professionally, no.
BLAKE:	But you were on the set for one of *my* favourite gay films, *Love Is Love*.
CLAY:	I was! I played the snarky caterer in the scene where Bryce Dallas Howard finds out that Tom Holland is gay.
BLAKE:	She deserved her Best Supporting win that year.
CLAY:	You know, I was chatting with Tom between takes. He was the one person on set who didn't think I was literally a caterer.
BLAKE:	A class act. His Golden Globe speech made me weep. I felt so seen.
CLAY:	You know, he was nervous about his sex scene.
BLAKE:	Nervous? But he was Spiderman!

---

[2] This can be changed to be any Edward Norton movie.

CLAY:	I know. But even Spiderman gets nervous when it comes to getting dong-adjacent with another actor.

BLAKE:	Stars. They're just like us.

CLAY:	He told me that he was dedicating his performance to his bisexual uncle.

BLAKE:	Well, what did you tell him?

CLAY:	I told him what I'm going to tell you all today. Are you worried about portraying the mechanics and realities of gay sex accurately on screen? Don't be. Because your director isn't.

Music plays as a NARRATOR announces the title of a new scene:

Modern Family: Going Full Costco With Your Life-Bro

CLAY:	The gay couple from *Modern Family.**

BLAKE:	The gay couple from *Schitt's Creek.**

CLAY:	The gay couple from *Glee.**

BLAKE:	The gay couple from *Shameless.**

CLAY:	Playing gay isn't just about portraying a character. It's about portraying a couple.

BLAKE:	Sometimes people assume that gay couples are different from our straight counterparts. That we're cut from a different, more *sequined* cloth.

CLAY:	But gay couples aren't much different than you and your girlfriend.

BLAKE:	Straight people may have invented couple-hood, but us gays have perfected it!

CLAY: We also have standard couple moments. Like, I don't know—

BLAKE: Yeah, like...

CLAY: Like when you show up to your boyfriend's ex's solo dance show only to find out that he's had sex with literally everyone there.

BLAKE: Yes! Or when you and your girlfriend take a quiet walk along the beach boardwalk...to cruise for anonymous sex.

CLAY: Just the other day my partner and I treated ourselves to a couples' massage. And when the towel-twinks asked us if we wanted a happy ending, I told them that being with Derek is the only happy ending I need.

BLAKE: How is Derek taking the breakup?

CLAY: Oh, not well.

BLAKE: And you still opted for the happy ending?

CLAY: It's important to support small businesses.

BLAKE: As you can see, us homos aren't so different from you heteros.

CLAY: Public-facing gay men have always made a point to tone down the gay.

BLAKE: In an effort to not scare off the general public.

CLAY: De-limping the wrists.

BLAKE: Lowering your voice.

Clay   Talking to your father.

BLAKE: Using poppers to actually clean your VCR.

CLAY: It's called *Buttigieging.*

BLAKE: Take Chasten Buttigieg. When marrying presidential hopeful Pete Buttigieg, Chasten took his last name. And given their neutered sex appeal, it's the *only* part of Pete that he's taking.

CLAY: Performing normalcy is an evolutionary protection for gays. So for Chasten, it was easy to play the role of *supportive wife.*

BLAKE: I'm so excited for this next part.

CLAY: We're going to present you with a scenelet from an exciting new screenplay called *Love, Chasten.* Written by a good friend of mine named Blake.

BLAKE: And co-written by a good friend of *mine* named Clay.

                  An instrumental cover of "Fast Car" plays while the boys don a set of cardigans. Music continues to play as a NARRATOR announces the title of a new scene:

Love, Chasten: A Gay Fantasia On National Themes

CLAY: We open on a ferry carrying Presidential hopeful Pete Buttigieg and his fiancé, Chasten. A couple with a newborn baby sits near. Our heroes look on with a reserved yearning.

BLAKE: Pete, I'm so happy we're finally getting away. A weekend at the New England Antique Festival is just what we need to put the spice back into our relationship.

CLAY: You're right. I can't wait to close-mouth kiss you on the Adirondacks.

BLAKE:	I've been saving this for Drag Brunch, but I might as well tell you now. We've been together for so long that I find myself slipping into a routine, you know?
CLAY:	Oh honey, it's like you're reading my mind. Somehow our L.L. Bean sweater sets aren't bringing us together the way they used to. It's almost like we need a third in our life. Maybe even a fourth.
BLAKE:	Pete?
CLAY:	Chasten?
BLAKE:	I've found a surrogate for our twins!

"Fast Car" swells and they lean dramatically into an almost-kiss that turns into a business-like handshake. End scene.

BLAKE:	The Buttigiegs batted a hundred and played a perfect game of gay parenting. One boy, one girl, and one sponsorship deal with Tide Detergent. Just what every family needs.
CLAY:	Neil Patrick Harris? Twins.
BLAKE:	Elton John? Twins.
CLAY:	Lance Bass? Twins.
BLAKE:	Matt Bomer? Twins.
CLAY:	Ricky Martin? Twins.[3]
BLAKE:	Proof that we can, and *will*, have a family that looks just like yours. Because you don't have to try and act like us. Not when we've been trying to act like you.

---

[3] If any other gay couples in the public eye have been added to this list, you may add them here.

Music plays as a NARRATOR announces the title of a new scene:

More Than A Victim: Adversity for the Un-Adversed

CLAY: We come now to my favourite part of the seminar. Blake and I are going to give you all a little test.

BLAKE: We're going to give you some scenarios.

CLAY: All *you* have to do is tell us how you would respond in these hypothetical situations.

BLAKE: You can trust us. We know a thing or two about getting tested.

BLAKE & CLAY play a game of multiple choice with their audience. The scene is improvised based around what answers the audience gives. The NARRATOR reads the situation while one of the boys steps forward to perform the act of oppression that goes along with it. The other leads the audience in guessing, before revealing the correct answer.

NARRATOR: *Being Denied A Bank Loan*

BLAKE: I'm sorry Mister Suckarowski. Focus on the Family Loans and Exchange doesn't give mortgages to couples of your sort. You and your...*roommate* can see yourselves out.

                   A: Our money is as good as anyone else's!

                   B: We refuse to be treated this way!

                   C: This is discrimination!

                   D: Thank you for your time.

                   Correct Answer: D

NARRATOR: *The Bartender Doesn't Take Kindly to Your Type Around Here*

CLAY: We don't carry no Smirnoff Ice 'round these parts, buster. Why don't you and your fitted jeans go back to New York City where you came from?

A: I didn't want to drink whatever horse piss is on tap here anyway.

B: Let's get out of here, Lance.

C: This is discrimination!

D: Thank you for your time.

Correct Answer: D

NARRATOR: *Getting Fired from Your Teaching Job*

BLAKE: There have been some complaints from the parents. *Heather Has Two Mommies* was not on the approved reading list. We're going to have to let you go, Mister Suckarowski.

A: Queer perspectives in the classroom are valid and important!

B: Consider the message that you're sending to queer students!

C: This is discrimination!

D: Thank you for your time.

Correct Answer: D

NARRATOR: *Getting Kicked Out of the House by Your Dad*

CLAY: You get out of my house! Your grandfather didn't win the Vietnam War for you to dress like some namby-pamby princess. You're no Suckarowski. You're not even my son.

A: I *am* your son, Dad! And I love you, even if you make it difficult sometimes.

B: This is who I am, and you can't treat me like this!

C: This is discrimination!

D: I'm leaving, and you'll never see me again!

Correct Answer: B

NARRATOR: *Being Told by the Toronto Police That There Is No Serial Killer in the Gay Village*

BLAKE: There is no serial killer in The Village. Those missing men simply moved to the suburbs.

A: Eight men have gone missing from The Village, and you're refusing to protect us.

B: Your Chief of Police blamed our community for the killings during a press conference by saying that we should have come forward sooner.

C: You're knowingly endangering the lives of queer people despite clear evidence that a pervy Mall Santa with a documented history of violence towards gay men is responsible.

D: You are standing by while he rapes and murders gay men, dismembers their bodies, and buries them on the grounds of his landscaping clients. We are not making this up.

Trick question, because the answer is:

E: Thank you for your time.

Music plays as a NARRATOR announces the title of a new scene:

Finding the Faggotry!

CLAY: While filming the 2014 war film *Fury*, Shia LaBeouf stopped bathing, pulled out his own tooth, and spent days watching videos of horses being shot.

BLAKE: While starring in Marvel's *Morbius*, Jared Leto walked around the set with crutches. He eventually stopped walking altogether and forced unsuspecting production assistants to bring him to the bathroom in a wheelchair.

CLAY: To film *The Machinist*, Christian Bale lost sixty-five pounds from eating only a single apple every day.

BLAKE: Dustin Hoffman.

CLAY: Acting is reacting. Reacting to a non-stop barrage of horse shootings. But to get over your hetero-dependency, you're going to need more than just a loop of Seabiscuit getting his brain blasted across the pavement.

BLAKE: You're going to need to dig deep to bring home prestige parts and a golden statue.

CLAY: These are actors with the time and resources to traumatize themselves into stardom. So how do the rest of us get into character without a wheelchair and a suicide diet?

BLAKE: By following the teachings of Blake & Clay! So join us as we give you the key to unlocking your inner gay!

CLAY: Tricks. They're not just how I paid my way through my twenties. They're also just what you need to get gay in no time at all.

BLAKE: Let's walk through some easy to remember techniques.

Music from a 60s-era educational film plays while the boys don a pair of cheeky ball caps, becoming Bradly and Brian.

NARRATOR: This is Bradly and Brian. They've never glanced at a penis, not even their own! But today they're Finding Their Faggotry! Say hi, boys!

They wave.

No, no. Not like that! A gay wouldn't be caught dead with a wrist quite so firm.

CLAY: Really?

BLAKE: Sure, Brian! My pop beat the "gay wave" out of me. He didn't like how happy I seemed waving goodbye to Grandma.

NARRATOR: Exactly! There's nothing gayer than living under constant fear of heterosexual violence.

The boys drop their wrists and let their hands flop.

NARRATOR: Now you're getting it! Let's say your pal has just told you something real swell. Something top notch and exciting! How do you react?

BLAKE: Cool, man.

CLAY: Way to go.

BLAKE: Good on ya!

NARRATOR: Now, boys! Is that really how you think a prancing fancy-lad would react to getting tickets for the latest female pop sensation? Or a brand-new pair of loafers?

BLAKE: Gee. I guess not.

CLAY: I hope that poofta isn't too light in his loafers, because he's going to need them to run away from the local hooligans who are just blowing off some steam!

BLAKE: Pop always says: *boys will be boys!*

NARRATOR: Darn tootin', boys. To find *your* gay, you're going to need to bring things up a notch. Or should I say, up an octave?

CLAY: But isn't using our full vocal register a sign of weakness and vulnerability?

BLAKE: Pop always says that a real man never raises his voice above an F-sharp 4.

NARRATOR: And a real man doesn't! But we're not talking about *real* men. We're talking about the gays.

             They both squeal a high-pitched scream.

             Now you're getting it! Let's say your best gal pal hands you a piping hot cup of joe. Show the folks at home how you react.

CLAY: Coffee? I love a cup of coffee.

BLAKE: Don't talk to me before I've had my morning coffee!

             They turn and share a canned laugh.

NARRATOR: There you go! The gays love their coffee.

BLAKE: Do they? Pop always says that a strong cup of black coffee is the last true bastion of real masculinity.

CLAY: A strong cup of black coffee and crying alone in the toolshed.

NARRATOR: Remember, the gays don't drink their coffee like you and I.

BLAKE: You mean they drink it with their butt?

CLAY: No, Brian! They drink it with their gal pals while discussing their latest erotic misadventures.

NARRATOR: No, boys. They drink it like fops and dandies have drunk coffee for ages. With their pinkies out! Try it yourself!

The boys pop their pinkies to a "ding" sound effect.

BLAKE: Wow! I'm getting gayer by the second!

CLAY: Put a bow on my backside and call me Fanny. I've never felt gayer!

BLAKE: It's a shame that Pop isn't here to see this. Not that he could see much after the mine collapsed. Pop always said that a real man enters a woman without protection and enters a mineshaft with even less. Real men pull ore from the earth with nothing but their bare hands and God's will. Did God allow that mine shaft to collapse? Did God allow Pop to be trapped for weeks, eating his foreman's body to survive? Maybe God wasn't there that day. Maybe this town truly is a place that Christ has turned away from. Pastor Jacobs said as much towards the end. Of course, it's not what Pastor Jacobs said. It's what he didn't say. Secrets have a way of building up around a town like this. Building up until they collapse all around you. Pop? Can you hear me? Can you see me?

Beat.

CLAY: What?

BLAKE: Sorry, I had the sudden urge to do a monologue about my daddy issues.

CLAY: Wow, these tricks really are working!

                  *They high-five and music plays, as a
                  NARRATOR announces the title of a new
                  scene:*

Accountability: A Platform Is More Than Just a Runway

                  *Award show music and canned applause
                  plays. The two pretend to accept awards.*

                  *They speak from the same acceptance
                  speech.*

CLAY: Oh, my goodness, I can't believe this. They're
                  right, it is heavier than it looks!

BLAKE: I am standing here tonight as a proud queer
                  ally, planted firmly on the shoulders of giants.

CLAY: Aristotle. Oscar Wilde. Billy Porter. I say your
                  names.

BLAKE: Playing Mayor Pete Buttigieg was a challenge.

CLAY: But more than that, it was an opportunity.

BLAKE: Because every day on set I reminded myself
                  that I wasn't doing this movie for me.

CLAY: I was doing it for my gay nephew, Carter.

BLAKE: Go to bed, Carter!

CLAY: I want to thank Julie. My rock, my foundation,
                  my North Star.

BLAKE: The best public defender turned wife and
                  mother that a schmo like me could ever ask
                  for.

CLAY: Thank you to my wonderful co-star, Chris
                  Pratt!* I could not have asked for a better
                  Chasten.

BLAKE:	Thank you to Will Smith for bringing so much authenticity to the ghost of Marsha P. Johnson.
CLAY:	When Gus Van Sant asked me to take on this behemoth of a role—
BLAKE:	I called him and I said *Gus, you have to be crazy!*
CLAY:	But when Gus insisted that I was the only person for the part—
BLAKE:	I knew that it was because of my training at the hands of Blake & Clay.

Playout music kicks in.

CLAY:	This award tonight is for Blake & Clay!
BLAKE:	Who we were so lucky to have on set as our queer consultants—
CLAY:	At a sensible rate that can be easily negotiated by contacting them…
BOTH:	At www.blake&clay.com!

The music fades.

CLAY:	That acceptance speech was written by the same bot that wrote Netflix's *Heartstopper*.
BLAKE:	So, you've booked the part, you've won the award, and you've sashayed into the hearts of culturistas everywhere. How do you hold on to that feeling of one-sided puppy love? How do you maintain your hard-won status as gay glitterati?
CLAY:	Remind yourself that the first pride was a protest? Pressure your local representatives to reverse the blood ban? Mentor at-risk queer youth?

BLAKE: No.

CLAY: You reference *Paris Is Burning* in your *Vanity Fair* interview.

BLAKE: You spruce up your gym selfie with a Larry Kramer quote.

CLAY: And you do a TikTok* lip sync to your favourite scene from *Will & Grace*.

BLAKE: It's called putting in the work.

CLAY: Blake, if you're watching a straight man accept an award for playing queer, what are you looking to see?

BLAKE: We're looking for the three Rs: Representation, Reverence, and Responsibility.

CLAY: These three guideposts will take your moment in the public eye from "paying lip service" to "servicing the queer community."

BLAKE: Representation is a matter of seeing ourselves portrayed accurately and positively.

CLAY: Remember that you're speaking for an entire community while you're up there. Delete the old tweets. Don't get political. And keep those dang hands to yourself! After all, the face of a movement can't have a blemish!

BLAKE: Reverence is about giving respect where it is due.

CLAY: Projections show that by 2045, everyone will have a gay nephew named Carter.

BLAKE: So thank Carter for all he's done by bringing him along as your plus one. Because saying our names is one thing, but saying our names on the red carpet of the GLAAD Awards is another thing entirely.

CLAY: Speaking of the red carpet, let me ask you one age-old question.

             The two pretend to be on a red carpet.

             "Who are you wearing?"

BLAKE: "I'm wearing a classic Keith Haring print and an Alexander McQueen-inspired jockstrap."

CLAY: A lot of people are going to accuse you of putting on queerness like a fancy cape. One that you can take off and hang up when it's convenient.

BLAKE: But this is a cape you won't find in the closet of one Harry Styles.

CLAY: Because when you're on the red carpet, you're going to be working that second R by giving Reverence to the culture that cultivated your red-hot red carpet success.

BLAKE: At the end of the day, reverence just means that you're including queer folk in the conversation.

CLAY: Yes! And sure, you might be the one actually *having* the conversation—

BLAKE: Making the money—

CLAY: Gaining the social capital—

BLAKE: But if us queers have learned anything while living beneath a system of violence and oppression...

             They both blank. The energy in the room flatlines. They stay in this silence for an uncomfortable amount of time before trying to get back on track.

> *BLAKE & CLAY speak rapidly, cutting off each other's lines.*

BLAKE: It's about accountability, right—

CLAY: Yes. And calling *in*, not calling *out*—

BLAKE: Making sure that we feel seen—

CLAY: Represented—

BLAKE: That our younger selves—

CLAY: That our younger selves are being spoken to—

BLAKE: That the heterosexual actors are speaking to the younger selves of the gay men watching them—

CLAY: That we see ourselves being seen by the straight people seeing us while they see the gay audience seeing them seeing us being seen.

BLAKE: Totally.

> *A pause.*

We come now to the cornerstone of this section, the glittering jewel in the tiara of representation.

CLAY: Responsibility.

BLAKE: Responsibility is about realizing the ways that you've been benefiting from the heterosexual worldview.

CLAY: It's about holding space without taking up space, and recognizing that queerness is not a costume.

BLAKE: It's about readjusting, reacclimating, reintegrating…

BLAKE loses the thread, CLAY tries to compensate. BLAKE & CLAY speak rapidly, cutting off each other's lines.

CLAY: Providing us space that is couched in living our lived experience—

BLAKE: I'm sorry. What are we asking them to do again, exactly?

CLAY: We're asking them to untangle their understandings in a way that invites us to un-live our traumas, un-trigger our internalized queer crises, and un—

BLAKE: I mean I have no idea what *I'm* supposed to do with any of this, let alone an entire audience of straight people. Like, are we holding them responsible for every drop of trauma that queer people have suffered?—

CLAY: It's about interrogating internal biases about how the 2SLGBTQIA+ experience has been rewritten by heteronormative dominance—

BLAKE: And *which* queer people? Like, all of them? We keep talking about queer people as if we're a monolith, and isn't that a problem on its own?—

CLAY: You'll be providing a platform for queer performers to benefit from—

BLAKE: I can only be responsible for myself. I can only answer for myself. I can only talk about how tired *I* am of fighting, how left behind *I* feel—

CLAY: Platforming our platform while de-platforming people who are un-platforming underrepresented peoples—

BLAKE: Because it's not like I was ever representing anyone in the first place, I was only ever trying to represent myself—

CLAY: When we talk about representation, what we're really talking about is—

BLAKE: When I was younger, I was too butch to book any of the bitchy receptionists or GAP associates or demon twinks that passed for representation. And I took that as a compliment. I wanted to work, sure, but at least I could pass. And I held onto that for a long time. Like I was achieving something by not getting tossed out of the room the second they caught wind of a notable lisp. And I kind of hate myself for that. But this is about you, right?

It's about you. Even though everyone is calling for authenticity and sensitivity. But I guess that stops at asking if you've ever had a dick in your mouth.

We really do want to eat our cake, don't we? Let's be authentic and open-hearted and create a safe working environment while we keep the faggots from booking. Because most of us aren't getting cast as gay, which means we're certainly not getting cast as straight.

And everything for the gays is a tender-hearted coming-of-age romance, so I'm not getting that call either. Because who wants to see anybody my age falling in love? I didn't think this seminar was going to be any good, but nobody cares if anything is *good* anymore. All we talk about is how important things are. How *vital* it is to see queer people on the screen. Even if the writers and actors and directors are all gold-star heteros.

CLAY: Folks, Blake is just going through something right now. He got some bad news last week, and—

BLAKE: But you people don't want complicated queers. You want queers who make space for you on the Pride float. You want to look like us. Which is to say that you want *us* to .look like *you.* I've spent my life trying to look like you. I've been contorting myself into whatever box you want to put me in, and it's given me a bad back and pinched nerves and failed relationships.

I can be the correct kind of gay, right? He's a bit rough around the edges. But that's what you like about him. His pinky doesn't stick out when he drinks his pint. And he *does* drink pints. He's rude, but it's endearing. He's cultured, but he's not loud about it. He's sexy, but not sexual. Why can't I play that? And I felt stupid, really, when I realized that the kind of gay I've been trying for isn't gay at all. It's you.

You bought queerness off the clearance rack and now you're selling it back to us so we can squabble over the pieces.

Let's make sure the gay characters are good people. Let's make sure they're intersectional. Even if they're being played by a guy with a wife and two kids. Even if the money from the Representation Industrial Complex hasn't once paid my rent. Let's put on a nice morality play with clearly marked exits and enough content warnings to kill an elephant. And don't speak for someone else. But don't not speak for someone else. Include the gays, but don't do it because you have to. But you *do* have to. And write us authentically. But not *too* authentically. Write us aspirationally. Write around our rough edges, please.

My agent dropped me last week.

BLAKE leaves the stage. CLAY considers his options before:

CLAY: I have this story I tell sometimes.

I was in theatre school, and my teacher told me that I wasn't going to get anywhere until I learned to speak in a lower tone and play straight as my default. For my own good, he said. And he wasn't wrong. But I tell this story at parties and with other actors and I always make sure to turn my gay voice up as high as it can go. To limp my wrists accordingly. But once my one-man show is over, all I can think about is the fact that I *did*. I did play straight as my default. I did play straight as my default. Until I learned that casting is always looking to fill the part of a waiter named Stevonne with limp wrists and a high voice.

But queer is in vogue now. So I joke that we're so popular I'm going to have to start teaching the straights how to play gay.

I'm not getting cast as the leading man. The husband. The womanizer. If I'm lucky I'll get cast as Hairdresser with One Line. Best Friend with One Line. Hate Crime Victim with One Line.

But the gays are stepping out of the background and taking the spotlight! And on a good day, I like to think that I bravely blazed this path for us. Those characters might have been *all* we had, but they were mine. And it wasn't hard to love them, because it wasn't hard to understand them. They were in the background, but they were the funniest person in the room. They stood tall while the straights talked over them, and if that's not the gay experience then I don't know what is.

I always thought about the little gay boys at home who might be watching. And I hoped they were paying attention. It's easy to look down at it now. But I played those parts because the only way forward was *through*. And now it seems that we are through.

I just didn't know that the cost of admission would be passing the flaming baton to you. I never thought you'd be meeting us at the gate to say, "Thanks so much, we'll take it from here."

And then I think *at least I'll always have my queer community.* And I really did think that. Until I learned that I'm the old guard. The little gay boys were watching at home. And now that they think about it, they're not very happy with me.

I was too queer for the mainstream, and now I'm too mainstream for the queer revolution. Being gay was always a liability, but now I'm not enough. Not young enough. Not queer enough, not straight enough. I'm in a grey area. And there's no grey on the pride flag.

BLAKE returns holding his phone. CLAY is unsure how to proceed.

BLAKE: When I was backstage I got some news.

CLAY: Okay.

BLAKE: We sold our screenplay.

CLAY: *Love, Chasten?*

BLAKE: It's going to Hollywood, baby!

Gay scream.

CLAY: I thought it had been passed over by every-one in town!

BLAKE: I'll say to you what I said to Kathryn Hahn when she had me forcibly removed from the set of *A Bad Moms Christmas*. You can't keep a good thing down! And I loved you in *Transparent*.

CLAY: And just when I was thinking of moving to the suburbs.

BLAKE: Here's the best part. They want us to play the Buttigieges'...elderly neighbours.

CLAY: Do I smell Baked Alaska?

BLAKE: I've got a hard candy for you right here, honey!

CLAY: Who do they have playing Pete and Chasten?

BLAKE: It's not confirmed—

CLAY: Okay.

BLAKE: But it's looking like Tom Holland* and the guy from *Love, Simon*.*

CLAY: Wow...they couldn't get Chalamet?

BLAKE: They tried, but he's still crying in front of that fireplace like it's the last night of Hanukkah.

CLAY: Well, folks, I hope you learned a lot today! I know we sure did.

BLAKE: I learned that representation on screen can't always be a one-to-one casting choice, but that you should always keep trying...to get one of the Spidermen as your lead.

CLAY: I learned that identity politics are a complex and multifaceted issue that can't be easily summed up in an hour-long seminar. It's best left for the experts...like Harry Styles and your gay nephew Carter.

BOTH: Go to bed, Carter!

CLAY: But mostly we learned to never sell out!

BLAKE: Never compromise!

CLAY: Stand firm in your truth!

BLAKE: Your lived experience!

CLAY: Your identity.

             They turn to leave, talking over each other as they go.

BLAKE: I think it's important that our craft services be done by a queer restaurant.

CLAY: How do we make sure the dogs are gay?

BLAKE: Twinks are underrepresented in the Grip community.

CLAY: What about that band Dua Lipa? We should ask them to sing our love ballad.

BLAKE: We should get Tony Kushner as our script supervisor.

CLAY: We are dedicating this movie to essential workers.

             They're gone, still talking from offstage.

             End of play.

Blake & Clay's Gay Agenda

Characters

BLAKE & CLAY are middle-aged gay men. Clay is older than Blake.

Accompanying Blake & Clay is the pre-recorded voice of a NARRATOR. It should be voiced by a man and delivered with the cadence of the narrators from a 1950s instructional film, particularly the work of Coronet Films.

DAN LEVY is the co-creator and co-star of *Schitt's Creek*, and he appears on stage in voice only. He is usually performed with pre-recorded vocal clips cued by the stage manager, but an offstage performer could also voice him in real time.

The vocal performance may sound just like the real-life Dan Levy, but it may also bear no resemblance to him at all.

DEREK is Clay's ex, and he appears on stage in voice only. As with Dan Levy, this should be performed by a man and can be pre-recorded or done live.

Setting

This play is simply a book launch that takes place on whichever stage it is literally being performed on. Perhaps there are two chairs or stools, otherwise the stage is bare. There is no fourth wall. The performers may deviate from the script to chat and improvise with the audience based on what is really happening in the room at the time. A common example of this during the original run was when Blake & Clay would welcome latecomers and catch them up on what they had missed.

The original production of *Blake & Clay's Gay Agenda* made use of a projector and screen to provide scene titles, text, visual aids, and sight gags. They are entirely optional. A few projections used in the original production have been noted and can be used or disregarded.

A Note on References

The music used in the original production is noted throughout. Song choices are merely suggestions and can be used as written or disregarded.

An asterisk* appears over people, places, or things that are local to the original staging of this text. These references should be replaced with whatever your local or national equivalent is. Asterisks also appear over the names of celebrities and social media platforms which should be updated with the times as you see fit.

Blake & Clay's Gay Agenda. Blake (Jonathan Wilson) and Clay (Daniel Krolik) discuss their incendiary new play. Photo by Kevin Connery, 2023.

Blake & Clay's Gay Agenda. Clay (Daniel Krolik) tells the audience about an exciting new concept he recently created. Photo by Kevin Connery, 2023.

NARRATOR: Please welcome to the stage the stars of your sister-in-law's favourite TV show! The jewel of Canadian television that launched a thousand quirky throw pillows! Disliking this sitcom juggernaut is an act of homophobia! From *Schitt's Creek*: Dan Levy and Noah Reid!

BLAKE & CLAY pop their heads on stage, slowly walking out.

BLAKE: We really should have cut that voiceover.

CLAY: So sorry, everyone! Dan and Noah are just running a bit late...to responding to our invitation.

BLAKE: They are such trailblazers.

CLAY: Representation wins.

BLAKE: Simply the best.

CLAY: Dan proved that all you need to make it in television is perseverance and a positive attitude.

BLAKE: It was his perseverance that got Dan his pitch with the CBC.

CLAY: And his positive attitude that convinced Catherine O'Hara to co-star.

BLAKE: I'm Blake.

CLAY:	I'm Clay.
BLAKE:	And you're—
BOTH:	Gay!
CLAY:	Just a gaggle of queers.
BLAKE:	A real bunch of bent buggers.
CLAY:	Residents of Chromatica.
BLAKE:	A pack of pansies.
CLAY:	A bakery full of fruit cakes.
BLAKE:	Oscar aficionados.
CLAY:	You're here because you heard the exciting news.
BLAKE:	We've been sitting on this one for a while.
CLAY:	And we know a thing or two about sitting on things.
BLAKE:	Clay and I are actors, writers, and change-makers.
CLAY:	Lovers, fighters, and community ambassadors.
BLAKE:	We're no stranger to queer history. We were even around for some of it.
CLAY:	Bathhouse raids.
BLAKE:	Don't Ask, Don't Tell.
CLAY:	Prop Eight.
BLAKE:	Angela Lansbury's workout video.
CLAY:	But today isn't just about our gay history. It's about our gay future.

BLAKE: Sure, things may seem perfect for us gays. Gay marriage.

CLAY: Gay divorce.

BLAKE: An entire month of Pride.

CLAY: Infinite *Drag Race* franchises.

BLAKE: But the truth is that our community is more divided than ever.

CLAY: Factions abound.

BLAKE: Generational divides.

CLAY: People who say they're "Gay, Not Queer."

BLAKE: "LGB without the T."

CLAY: Gays against drag.

BLAKE: Kink at pride.

CLAY: Cops at pride.

BLAKE: Sexual racism.

CLAY: Regular racism.

BLAKE: Infinite *Drag Race* franchises.

CLAY: What we need now is unity.

BLAKE: A set of standards we can all agree on.

CLAY: So just as Moses came down from the mountain with his Commandments—

BLAKE: How many were there?

CLAY: Historians say there's no way to know.

BLAKE: We, too, come bearing a new batch of words to live, laugh, and love by.

> *They reveal a book:* Blake & Clay's Gay Agenda.

> Compiled here, in a little something I wrote with a good friend of mine named Clay.

CLAY: Decreed here in this paradigm-shifting, life-changing compendium that I wrote with a good friend of mine named Blake.

BLAKE: It's a simple set of standards—

CLAY: Ideas—

BLAKE: And principles—

CLAY: Intended to finally unite the gay community.

BOTH: And we think you're really gonna go for it.

CLAY: It's a sexy—

BLAKE: But informative—

CLAY: Set of standards that us gays can hold ourselves to.

BLAKE: It'll be the first book you've read since you tried to find the sex scenes in *Heartstopper*.

CLAY: I wrote this guide after delving into my own lived experience as an out and proud gay man. Thinking back on years of triumph, hardship, and above all, love.

BLAKE: And I wrote this guide beneath the comfort of a weighted blanket, recalling that time I went to a gay bar in 2005.

CLAY: *Blake & Clay's Gay Agenda* is about to go on sale, but we're here to offer you a comprehensive tour of its interior.

BLAKE: Like Clay does every Friday night at Steamworks Bathhouse.*

CLAY: The Gay Agenda is a cheat sheet for the eternal pop quiz that is gay life.

BLAKE: It's an exciting time to be gay. We are living proof that there are countless ways to be, think, and live gay. Proof that there really are infinite gay identities.

CLAY: Which we've compressed into an easy to read forty-six pages.

BLAKE: So join us, as we open the cover—

BOTH: To Blake & Clay's Gay Agenda!

Music plays as a NARRATOR announces the title of the next scene:

Normalizing Gay Sex: From Vanilla to Rocky Road

BLAKE: Gay men sure have come a long way in the boardroom *and* in the bedroom.

CLAY: We once were forced to have sex in parks, back alleys, and truck stop bathrooms.

BLAKE: And now we choose to have sex in parks, back alleys, and truck stop bathrooms.

CLAY: Gay sexuality is a political act. And I got political four times last week.

BLAKE: Which means that we can never take our sexual freedom for granted.

CLAY: Exactly. We have to take advantage of our hard-earned rights. Which I do by keeping a long-standing biweekly threesome.

BLAKE: Yes! Or kissing.

CLAY: Eating ass.

BLAKE: Cuddling.

CLAY: Double penetration.

BLAKE: Hugging.

CLAY: Golden showers.

BLAKE: Talking.

CLAY: Fisting.

BLAKE: A good back rub.

CLAY: Electing yourself bukkake king of the city and slowly transforming into a sexually liberated slime monster.

BLAKE: To live in a gay body is to inhabit centuries of sexual repression, misrepresentation, and a little something I'm sure every gay understands.

BOTH: Shame.

BLAKE: Let's see a show of hands. Who here has ever felt sexual shame?

               BLAKE & CLAY wait to see who has responded and riff accordingly.

CLAY: None of us is beyond shame. Just last week I hooked up with a gym trainer who had never seen *Hello, Dolly!*

BLAKE: And on the odd occasion I find myself having sex, it's interrupted by visions of my ancestors in the Holocaust.

CLAY: Now folks, *I'm* a bit of a freak. But Blake is a bit of a meek.

BLAKE: Guilty as charged.

CLAY: *Blake & Clay's Gay Agenda* challenges us all to release our sexual shame. So I challenged Blake to break out of his shell. Let his freak flag fly! Explore fertile new grounds like an erotic Lewis and Clark.

BLAKE: Were they having sex in those mountains?

CLAY: In the words of Michelle Williams, they didn't go up there to fish.

BLAKE: I was definitely stepping out of my comfort zone. But *Blake & Clay's Gay Agenda* has helped me recognize that our comfort zones were imposed on us by a heteronormative worldview.

CLAY: Which is why I rented Blake a room at our local bathhouse. I left him with nothing but a bottle of Gatorade, some K-Y Jelly, and a sexual checklist. Let's take a look at the results.

            The checklist is read by the NARRATOR and may also appear on screen.

NARRATOR: *Flirt with an Older Man*

BLAKE: His name was Abraham, and I later found out he was the janitor.

NARRATOR: *Rub Chests with Someone of Selleckian Proportions*

BLAKE: His name was Abraham, and I later found out he was the janitor.

NARRATOR: *Turn Your Rented Room into a Sexual Clown Car*

BLAKE: All I had to do was get my phone and play bootleg footage of Beanie Feldstein in *Funny Girl.*

NARRATOR: *Clamps*

BLAKE: Cramps.

NARRATOR: *Pain*

BLAKE: A constant existential dread.

NARRATOR: *Rubber*

BLAKE: I hardly know her.

NARRATOR: *Restraints*

BLAKE: Yes, I exercised a lot of restraint.

NARRATOR: *Gags*

BLAKE: Only a couple of pratfalls.

NARRATOR: *Successfully Having Sex Without Thinking About Your Ancestors*

BLAKE: Yes! Nothing but some faint klezmer music!

CLAY: So you reach the end of the checklist. The shame has melted from you, along with various bodily fluids. Blake, what was it like following *Blake & Clay's Gay Agenda* to sexual liberation?

BLAKE: There were so many people helping me along the way. I want to thank the dom top Otter who called me out for kink-shaming when I was too ashamed to act as his human urinal.

CLAY: Calling you in by calling you out.

BLAKE: I'd like to thank the rugged daddy Bear who spoke so eloquently on my internalized

homophobia when I declined to lie under his
glass table.

CLAY: We *have* to recognize the way the hetero-
            sexual hegemony has colonized our thought
            structures.

BLAKE: And a very special thank you to the gentleman
            who pointed out how repressed I was being
            when I refused to step on his balls with a pair
            of soccer cleats.

CLAY: Because refusing to lace up those soccer cleats
            was the product of the number one threat to
            gay liberation: shame. Because when we are
            repressed we are more likely to oppress.

            *Music plays as a NARRATOR announces
            the title:*

All in the Family: There's Nothing Wrong with Gay Rights

CLAY: It may seem like gay families finally have it
            all.

BLAKE: Equal parental rights between both partners.

CLAY: More countries opening up to gay adoption.

BLAKE: Increased visibility for families of all shapes
            and sizes.

CLAY: But that doesn't mean queer families aren't
            facing an uphill battle.

BLAKE: It doesn't mean there aren't still issues, both
            systemic and personal.

CLAY: While writing *Blake & Clay's Gay Agenda* we
            spoke to a wide range of LGBTQ+ families
            to discover their triumphs, but also their
            tribulations.

BLAKE: We amalgamated their experiences into a case study which we think really speaks their truth.

CLAY: To remind us that the fight is far from over.

> *The opening lines of Macklemore's "Same Love" play.*
>
> *BLAKE & CLAY each retrieve bottles of green juice with giant reusable straws.*
>
> *They are now Daxtonne and Archer, two regular teenage boys.*

CLAY: Hi! I'm Daxtonne.

BLAKE: And I'm Archer.

CLAY: We may be twins—

BLAKE: But we're just like you!

CLAY: The only difference?

BLAKE: Is that we have *two* dads!

CLAY: Just two regular, everyday Joes who wanted to settle down and raise a family.

> *They show pictures of their fathers. Both are gorgeous, ripped studs who live in a mansion and exude wealth.*

BLAKE: This is Paypay and Dayday.

CLAY: Our family may be a little different, but our parents are just like yours!

BLAKE: That's right! Our parents have regular jobs just like yours.

CLAY: Paypay is a former boy band member. He founded a line of alternative pajama sets that promote mental health.

BLAKE:	And Dayday is body positive on TikTok.*
BOTH:	Just like your parents.
CLAY:	They work a standard three-day work week.
BLAKE:	We're so lucky that our parents can work from any one of our homes.
BOTH:	Just like your parents.
CLAY:	Sometimes Dayday comes home late from work at 2:30 PM, exhausted from his weekly Instagram Live.*
BLAKE:	But we're always cared for by our au pair, Dillon. He has a BA in musical theatre.
CLAY:	Our parents may have set us up for success, but it's not always so easy. Sometimes we face discrimination for being part of a 2SLGBTQIA+ family.
BLAKE:	Just last week the server at Le Pain Quotidien used a coarse ground mustard on my prosciutto and dried fig sandwich, despite my request otherwise. Was it because I was seated with my two gay fathers? Yes.
CLAY:	Last year our fathers were accused of trying to bribe our way into Juilliard. Was it because their governing board didn't get the memo about what a modern family looks like? Yes.
BLAKE:	We booked Doja Cat* for our sixteenth birthday, but she cancelled at the last minute due to "extreme health issues" and "requiring invasive emergency surgery." But it's just like Paypay always says: when someone shows you who they are? Believe them.
CLAY:	But we don't let our struggles define us. It's not about queer trauma. It's about queer joy.

BLAKE: There are so many things about growing up with gay parents that make me feel joyful. Ask any child of a gay household and they'll tell you the same.

CLAY: Spreading La Mer on your toast every morning is an act of queer joy.

BLAKE: Our monthly tennis lesson with the Williams sisters is an act of radical queer joy.

CLAY: Hiring Joe Mantello to direct your Montessori school's production of *Dear Evan Hansen* is a subversive act of queer joy.

BLAKE: Getting Patti LuPone to lead three choruses of "Adon Olam" at your bar mitzvah is a selfless example of radical queer joy.

CLAY: Sponsoring a village in Africa isn't an act of queer joy. Queer joy is naming that village after your late Bichon Frisé.

BLAKE: It's just like Jonathan Van Ness* said: be the change you want to see in the world.

CLAY: Running a pajama empire can't be easy. Especially when you're trying to decolonize your business lingo.

BLAKE: But our parents take care of us the same way any parent would.

CLAY: By having that server at Le Pain Quotidien fired on the spot, before sending a video of the incident to a contact at *The Daily Beast*.*

BOTH: What any parent would do.

BLAKE: It's just what Dayday always says: It takes a village.

CLAY: And a chauffeur.

BLAKE:	And a publicist.
CLAY:	And a Mandarin tutor.
BLAKE:	Our parents are just like yours. They want only the best for us.
CLAY:	Which is why Paypay and Dayday signed us to a lifetime contract with Tide Detergent the moment we were born.
BLAKE:	Because Tide knows that families come in all shapes and sizes.
CLAY:	Use code PAYPAY to receive 25% off your next purchase of Tide PODS® Plus Febreze® Odor Defense.
BLAKE:	Because what really smells? Is intolerance.

Music plays as a NARRATOR announces the title:

Gay Mental Health: You Better Put in the Work, Bitch

BLAKE:	There's been a lot of talk recently about mental health.
CLAY:	Let's get a show of hands. Who here has mental health?
BLAKE:	You know, Clay, for the longest time I thought I was the only person in the world with mental health.
CLAY:	You're not alone, Blake. So many people experience mental health.
BLAKE:	That's why Clay and I feel so lucky to be advocating for gay mental health.
CLAY:	Gay men are a cornucopia of mental health issues.

BLAKE: Drug addiction.

CLAY: Alcoholism.

BLAKE: Oversexualization.

CLAY: Eating disorders.

BLAKE: And those are just the fun ones.

CLAY: Body dysmorphia.

BLAKE: Daddy issues.

CLAY: Mommy issues.

BLAKE: Poor self-esteem.

CLAY: Obsessive fixations.

BLAKE: Depression.

CLAY: Anxiety.

BLAKE: Being named Dillon and having a BA in musical theatre.

CLAY: Just last week I had a panic attack while re-watching Gwyneth Paltrow's Oscar speech.

BLAKE: You have to stop doing this to yourself.

CLAY: I go back and I think *maybe this time it'll be Cate Blanchett.*

BLAKE: Clay? I need you to hear me. You will get through this. We will get through this.

CLAY: To live as a gay man is to live with so much trauma.

BLAKE: I bet that's exactly how Glenn Close feels.

CLAY: What's something that makes you feel anxious, Blake?

BLAKE:	Jukebox musicals. You?
CLAY:	Women named Debra.
BOTH:	Yeah.
CLAY:	Let's delve into what taking care of *your* mental health can look like, now more than ever.
BLAKE:	It's a little something that we've been calling *self-care*.
CLAY:	Case in point: just last week I ran into my ex.
BLAKE:	How is Derek?
CLAY:	Oh, not well.
BLAKE:	Has he stopped crying onto your voicemail?
CLAY:	Mostly.
BLAKE:	How did it go?
CLAY:	Well, he stopped me on the street and he really laid into me. He said "you manipulated me, you constantly triggered my body dysmorphia, my eating disorders, my depression and anxiety, you made me feel like I would be nothing without you. And the worst part is that I still feel that way."
BLAKE:	Wow. That's a lot to hear.
CLAY:	Ultimately it was a good thing. Because I took in everything that Derek was saying. It was difficult, but I did owe him that. And after really considering what he'd said, I landed on a pretty major realization.
BLAKE:	Really?

CLAY:	I realized that...Derek isn't good for my mental health.
BLAKE:	That's huge.
CLAY:	Derek wanted me to self-care for *his* self, when I needed to be self-caring for *my* self.
BLAKE:	How did you respond?
CLAY:	I responded the way any mentally healthy person would. By getting myself a boba tea.
BOTH:	Self-care!
BLAKE:	We all live with a high degree of anxiety. It's impossible not to.
CLAY:	Soaring cost of living.
BLAKE:	Legislative violence against trans and queer people.
CLAY:	The return of fascism.
BLAKE:	Impending environmental collapse.
CLAY:	Sometimes it can feel like we have no control.
BLAKE:	And when things feel out of my control, I try to focus on the things I *can* control. Like my acting career.
CLAY:	That's great.
BLAKE:	For me, self-care looks like a night spent sending a series of emails to my agent detailing my career objectives.
CLAY:	And you've stopped crying onto her voicemail?
BLAKE:	Mostly.
BOTH:	Self-care. Important.

BLAKE: I find it most important to exercise self-care in moments when things aren't going my way. I recently lost out on a great role. Single pop culture obsessive Jewish gay man with a penchant for show tunes.

CLAY: Representation matters.

BLAKE: I had a very promising callback, but ultimately the role of Saul Rabinowitz was given to a recent graduate of St. William's Ecclesiastical College of Divinity and Musical Theatre.

CLAY: They have a very well-regarded BA program.

BLAKE: When I didn't get the part, I decided to follow up with the director. Just to see how I could improve next time.

CLAY: Any good feedback?

BLAKE: Apparently, I seemed "overly intellectual," "too New York," and I "carried the weight of my people's genocide too visibly."

CLAY: You do carry a lot of tension in your shoulders.

BLAKE: They also said I came across as "entitled." They said that I "refused to take direction," and that I "deviated drastically from the text."

CLAY: Last I checked, that was called *making choices*.

BLAKE: It was a rude awakening.

CLAY: About the antisemitism baked into the acting industry?

BLAKE: About how...I can't take those notes to heart. Because that is what? Self-care!

CLAY: So what did you do?

BLAKE: I drew myself a bath, grabbed my phone, and
                     you know what I ordered? A goddamn boba
                     tea.

CLAY: That's my girl!

BLAKE: Because there are so many people who are
                     going to bushel your candle. And it's up to
                     you to tell them:
                     1- You're wrong.
                     B- I'm perfect.
                     3- There is nothing I have to change about
                     myself.

                     *The boys lead the audience in repeating this
                     back to them.*

                     *CLAY's phone rings. He shows BLAKE
                     the screen.*

                     Oh my God, it's Derek! You need to pick
                     up that phone and tell him that he's wrong,
                     you're perfect, and there is nothing you need
                     to change about yourself.

CLAY: Are you sure?

BLAKE: Pick it up!

                     CLAY puts the phone on speaker mode.

CLAY: Go for Clay.

                     Derek's voice plays for everyone to hear.

DEREK: You're a fucking whore, Clay! And I'm going
                     to tell everyone what you're really like. I'm
                     going to ruin your life the way you ruined
                     mine. And if nobody believes me? I'm going
                     to kill myself at your front door. I'll do it, Clay,

I swear to God. And another thing! If I don't get my guinea pig returned by the end of the week—

CLAY hangs up. Neither moves, both totally shocked.

BLAKE: Oh my God. That was…total self-care!

"Fight Song" by Rachel Platten plays. They hug triumphantly.

Music plays as a NARRATOR announces the title:

Gays On Stage: From Chorus Boys to Chorus Men

BLAKE: Gay stories have made such an impact on our culture.

CLAY: *Brokeback Mountain.*

BLAKE: *Call Me by Your Name.*

CLAY: *Top Gun.*

BLAKE: A central tenet of *Blake & Clay's Gay Agenda* is to always use your platform to uplift queer stories.

CLAY: Our platform is the stage. And I've always said that theatre is storytelling.

BLAKE: It's not talked about enough, theatre is storytelling—

CLAY: And storytelling is theatre.

BLAKE: I knew that theatre was for me when eight-year-old Blake gifted his family a performance of "The Music and the Mirror" on day three of his grandmother's shiva.

CLAY: I knew that theatre was for me when a casting agent told me that I have the cheekbones for stage lighting.

BLAKE: Theatre isn't just for us. It's for every gay out there. Every sensitive, artistic, lonely little gay boy...who was passed over for Seymour Krelborn in the B'nai Brith Summer Camp production of *Little Shop of Horrors* for a hot lifeguard in Buddy Holly glasses.

CLAY: Exactly.

BLAKE: Which is why we're so excited to announce our commitment to developing new theatrical endeavours.

CLAY: We're calling it *Gay for Play*.

BLAKE: And we're currently seeking funding from a diverse series of granting bodies.

CLAY: Granting bodies with a commitment to championing underrepresented voices.

BLAKE: Finally, a space for two gay men to be onstage. A space to be unapologetically ourselves.

CLAY: It's been so liberating. I haven't apologized in weeks.

BLAKE: Because as *Blake & Clay's Gay Agenda* says:

CLAY: "We Will Storytell Our Own Storytellings."

BLAKE: Here for you now is *Gay for Play: A Theatrical Coming Out*.

             Music and NARRATOR announce each play title.

NARRATOR: *The Horse Is the Rider to the Blood and the Bone,* by Blake

BLAKE: This incendiary new play asks one bold question: what if someone was gay, but also lived on a farm?

CLAY: A gay teenage boy is uprooted from his life in the bustling city when his family relocates to a small farming town.

BLAKE: His crush on a local farmhand is complicated by the strange, biblical visions he begins to receive of a hunky angel with a really big dick.

CLAY: Just super hung.

BLAKE: Medically unsustainable.

CLAY: It's a metaphor for the patriarchy.

BLAKE: Through biblical imagery and graphic depictions of gay sex, *The Horse Is the Rider to the Blood and the Bone* asks one bold question hitherto unasked by contemporary theatre: can somebody hold two identities at once?

NARRATOR: *BRUNCH*, by Clay

CLAY: This incendiary new play examines gay bodies within gay time, gay space, and gay dining culture.

BLAKE: An unflinching deconstruction of the violence enacted on queer bodies by the heteronormative standards of mealtime.

CLAY: Brunch is not breakfast.

BLAKE: Brunch is not lunch.

CLAY: Brunch lives outside these rigid social structures.

BLAKE: Brunch challenges us to break down these gastronomical binaries.

CLAY: Part memoir, part dance, and part shadow puppetry, *BRUNCH* delves deep into the very process of creating theatre, implicating the audience by literally turning a camera on them at several points throughout the performance.

BLAKE: Clay will bravely perform his own play and stage act one in the very dressing room of the theatre you're watching it in.

CLAY: You thought performance begins when the actors step on stage?

BLAKE: Check your preconceived notions of theatrical norms at the door.

CLAY: Because if theatre audiences love one topic? It's theatre.

BLAKE: Through biblical imagery and graphic depictions of gay sex, *BRUNCH* asks one bold question: why am I being charged extra for half fries, half salad?

NARRATOR: *Bloodline*, by Blake

CLAY: In this autobiographical multidisciplinarium, trauma is a three-letter word: D-A-D.

BLAKE: *Bloodline* is a searingly honest exploration of my inheritances: male pattern baldness and male pattern trauma.

CLAY: Join Blake as he embodies the stories and traumas that have formed his queer identity, something never before attempted onstage. Stories like coming out to his father after Blake's adult tap dancing recital.

> *BLAKE affects a new character for each story, performing in the style of a classic one-man show.*

BLAKE:	"Before I shuffle out of your life forever, just know that there's not a thing about me that I will ever hop-flap-ball change."
CLAY:	His father's time as a cantor in training in 1960s Montreal.
BLAKE:	"But it's not *my* dream, Papa! It's yours. And the truth is that I put the can't in cantor."
CLAY:	His grandfather's time during a little something called the Holocaust.
BLAKE:	"Excuse me? Could I get a little salt with this gruel?"
CLAY:	And the sexual awakening of his first queer ancestor: a lowly shtetl goat farmer, torn between his love of the Torah and his love of the local milkman.
BLAKE:	"I love him, Yankel. What would you do if you were in my shoes?"
	A goat bleats.
	You're right, Yankel. Spoken with the wisdom of Solomon.
CLAY:	Through hats, wigs, and the swishing of a red scarf, Blake unpacks his lineage of trauma with song, dance, and a lot of audience interaction.
BLAKE:	*Bloodline* is an incendiary new play that asks one bold question: Papa, can you hear me?
NARRATOR:	*Fagamemnon*, by Blake and Clay
BLAKE:	This incendiary new play asks one bold question: what if there were gay people in Ancient Greece?
CLAY:	Set during the 2020 lockdown—

BLAKE: But also during the events of Agamemnon—

CLAY: This verbatim piece of physical dance theatre combines Greek myth with Blake's Grindr messages to create a vision of queer community that transcends time, space, and lockdown compliance.

BLAKE: What if Agamemnon was on Grindr?

CLAY: What if Clytemnestra was an anti-masker?

BLAKE: What if Aegisthus was hoarding toilet paper?

CLAY: What if Cassandra was a conspiracy theorist?

BLAKE: What if Medea refused to vaccinate her children?

CLAY: What if we banged pots and pans while wearing dance belts?

BLAKE: It was either this or an AIDS play set during The Plague.

CLAY: And my Fire Island Decameron is just *not* ready for workshop.

BLAKE: When we got out of lockdown, I said, "You know what contemporary theatre needs right now? Something vibrant, something fresh! Greek theatre."

CLAY: There's no biblical imagery, but are there graphic depictions of gay sex?

BLAKE: It's based on my Grindr profile, so no.

CLAY: We have been blessed with a platform to tell unflinching, uncompromising queer stories. And it's time that you found your platform to do the same.

BLAKE: Find *your* biblical imagery.

CLAY:	Find *your* thirty-five minutes of audience interaction.
BLAKE:	And tell our stories the way they were meant to be told.
BOTH:	While wearing dance belts.

Music plays as a NARRATOR announces the title of a new scene:

Gay Representation: Finding the Focus Group Within

Dark, moody film noir music plays. We hear the sound of rain.

BLAKE:	New York City, 1982.
CLAY:	The home of a subculture about to be ravaged by AIDS.
BLAKE:	Cut to a rain-soaked alleyway. Standing over the body of a dead rent boy is Taylor Thomas: Private Eye.
CLAY:	This is the third rent boy to show up dead this week. I smell hot garbage…and a pattern.
BLAKE:	You sure that's all you smell? Because I spilled poppers all over my penny loafers last night.
CLAY:	Thomas is joined by Detective Stanley McGriddle.
BLAKE:	They square off across the body with a charged eroticism.
CLAY:	You always were light in the loafers, McGriddle.
BLAKE:	It's not your *shoes* that I'm interested in, Taylor Thomas.

CLAY: When are you going to get it through those thick thighs of yours, McGriddle? The only privates you're going to be seeing tonight? Is this Private Eye in action.

BLAKE: A man can dream, can't he, Taylor Thomas? Well, not this man. Because he's dead.

CLAY: Dead and gay. In fact, these boys were all last seen exiting *Club Prolapse*.

BLAKE: The fisting bar?

CLAY: This boy was last seen playing puppet on Ventriloquist Night.

BLAKE: No strings attached. Just like a certain private eye.

CLAY: You know I don't do monogamy, McGriddle. I'm gay, and it's 1982.

BLAKE: Goddamnit, Taylor Thomas, why do these serial killings make me so horny?

CLAY: Because life is short, Griddy. As short as those shorts you wear to play squash at the West Village YMCA.

BLAKE: Life is short. And death is long. And *Cats* is now and forever.

CLAY: It's really nice to have Betty Buckley back on Broadway.

BLAKE: If only it had a stronger book.

CLAY: If only it had *any* book.

BLAKE: I know this case isn't easy, Taylor Thomas. Not after everything you went through as a young rent boy.

CLAY: This isn't about the past. This is about the future. Because we're looking at even more deceased nancy boys if we can't solve this case soon.

BLAKE: You're onto something, Taylor Thomas. The only person capable of this kind of horror is someone who knows a thing or two about our debauched, shameful lifestyle. A fellow gay man.

CLAY: You think this killer is a friend of Dorothy?

BLAKE: Dorothy Lamour? Or Dorothy Loudon?

CLAY: Exactly.

BLAKE: He must be a real puff pastry.

CLAY: A card-carrying knob-gobbler.

BLAKE: As gay as the day is gay.

They draw close, nearly kissing.

CLAY: Like I always say, McGriddle: you can't get to heaven on a levitating tire. Like in the musical *Cats*. In this instance heaven is my pants, and the levitating tire is—

BLAKE: Gunfire rings across the alleyway! Cutting short the final words of Taylor Thomas: Private Eye. He falls into the arms of the only man he ever truly loved: Stanley McGriddle.

           No! Don't you die on me, Taylor Thomas! Not when gay men have finally achieved liberation! Sure, we'll never be able to get gay married. But we're gay men in 1982 New York City, and we're going to live forever!

End scene.

CLAY: Thank you, everyone.

BLAKE: As some of you may know, Clay and I are a screenwriting duo.

CLAY: The scenelet you have just witnessed is from a developing TV pilot with the working title: *True Detective But Gay*.

BLAKE: We're promising to show one penis for every breast that appears on screen.

CLAY: Writing realistic and honest queer representation isn't something that we take lightly.

BLAKE: Last week we presented this scene to a queer-identifying focus group.

CLAY: Their opinions and lived experiences proved so vital to our creative process.

BLAKE: Did you know that queer people have a lot of opinions?

CLAY: And we are so proud to present for you the fruits of this emotional labour.

                Soft, inspirational music plays.

BLAKE: New York City, 1982.

CLAY: The home of a subculture about to be ravaged by inspiring stories of love and community.

BLAKE: Cut to a rain-soaked alleyway. Standing over the body of a deceased sex worker is Taylor Thomas: Private Eye.

CLAY: Let me just cover up this body. After all, a dead body could be triggering to anyone who missed the opening content warning.

BLAKE: It's like I always say: the following program contains implied violence, off-screen death, as well as depictions of trauma and fear.

CLAY: Thomas is joined by Detective Stanley McGriddle. They square off across the body with a charged...professional respect.

BLAKE: I see you made it here before me, Taylor Thomas. I'm glad, as I greatly respect your work as a fellow 2SLGBTQIA+ member of our field.

CLAY: I feel the same towards you. After all, when one of us succeeds, we all succeed.

BLAKE: I do wonder if depicting a sex worker as the victim of violence is reductive. After all, sex work is real work.

CLAY: You're right. I checked again. He's not a sex worker. He's a guidance counsellor.

BLAKE: A guidance counsellor who worked with at-risk queer youth?

CLAY: Of course.

BLAKE: So important.

CLAY: He was last seen exiting *Club Prolapse*.

BLAKE: The sex-positivity bar?

CLAY: This boy was last seen playing Puppet on Ventriloquist Night.

BLAKE: No strings attached. Just like a certain private eye.

CLAY: I practice ethical non-monogamy. My throuple is as valid as any monogamous relationship.

BLAKE: It is so valid.

CLAY: Valid as heck.

BLAKE: Goddamnit, Taylor Thomas, why do these serial killings always make me so sex-positive?

CLAY: I don't know, McGriddle. But I have no intention of kink-shaming you. Because life is short, and I'd never invalidate your sexuality that way.

BLAKE: Life is short. And death is long. And *Cats* is now and forever.

CLAY: I too enjoy musical theatre. But not in a way that could be read as stereotypical.

BLAKE: I know this case isn't easy for you, Taylor Thomas. Not after everything you went through as a young guidance counsellor.

CLAY: You're right, McGriddle. But my trauma doesn't define me. Not since I learned that mental health is real health.

BLAKE: You are strong. You matter. You are enough.

CLAY: Are you in the right headspace to receive some information that could possibly hurt you? Because I'm beginning to suspect that these killings are being committed by a serial killer of queer experience.

BLAKE: I thought the same thing, until I realized that a serial killer being 2SLGBTQIA+ is a harmful and homophobic trope.

CLAY: You're right. I checked again. The real killer here was institutional negligence.

BLAKE: Those bastards!

CLAY: Now that we've solved the case, I wondered if I might ask your consent to ask you on a date.

BLAKE: I consent.

CLAY: Would you like to go on a date?

BLAKE: Only if we hold pinkies while Troye Sivan* plays in the background.

CLAY: I literally don't know any other way.

BLAKE: Gunfire rings across the alleyway! But the would-be assailant misses, because killing a gay character is a harmful and homophobic trope.

CLAY: He is quickly apprehended by a team of trained community mediators.

BLAKE: And look! The guidance counsellor isn't dead! He was just taking a well-deserved nap.

BOTH: Self-care!

"Fight Song" by Rachel Platten plays. They hug triumphantly.

Music plays as a NARRATOR announces the title:

PRIDE: Putting the Unity in Community

CLAY: Pride week is a sacred time for us gays.

BLAKE: Like the Super Bowl half-time show.

CLAY: The Oscar nominations for Best Supporting Actress.

BLAKE: And seeing that your ex-boyfriend got fat.

CLAY:	Pride has lost some of its lustre over the last few years, hasn't it, folks?
BLAKE:	It's gotten so corporate.
CLAY:	So crowded.
BLAKE:	So many lines! And I'm not just talking about the coke.
CLAY:	But we saw something that reminded us of the importance of public visibility. We witnessed a young twink getting off the subway and seeing the marvel that was his first Pride parade.
BLAKE:	This haunted Victorian doll was sixteen, maybe seventeen. Right next to him was an older gentleman who must have been his father.
CLAY:	And I heard that twink say something that stuck with me. He said: "Pride really is amazing. I never knew I could feel so at home in a new place." That's what Pride should feel like. It should feel like home.
BLAKE:	They were joined by two elderly tweakers who proceeded to spit-roast that methy twink in the nearest alleyway.
CLAY:	But a family can look like anything. And at Pride? We're all family. What I saw in that alleyway inspired me to live Pride to the fullest.
BLAKE:	And what I saw in that alleyway inspired me to go home and order the Popeyes Family Feast.
CLAY:	Oddly enough, "Popeyes Family Feast" is the technical term for what happened in that alleyway.

BLAKE: During Pride celebrations, it's important to think about not only where we're going, but also to be reminded of where we are coming from.

CLAY: What would you say to eight-year-old... Blake?

            CLAY presents a photograph of a Victorian child.

BLAKE: I'd say, Blake, there will be times when you feel left out and alone. There will be times when you are out of step with what people are looking for in a gay man. There will be times when you're sitting at home, wondering if you've missed your last chance for true love or to find your chosen family.

            There is an uncomfortably long pause.

            Anyway! What would you tell eight-year-old Clay?

            BLAKE presents a painting of a 17th-century child in fancy royal garb.

CLAY: I would say to him...that on September eleventh, 2001, there will be a coordinated attack on the World Trade Center via hijacked planes leaving Logan International. And to always love himself.

BLAKE: Let's remind ourselves that the first Pride was a protest. Let's remind ourselves that Marsha P. Johnson threw the first brick at Judy Garland's funeral.

CLAY: Let's remind ourselves that Anita Bryant threw a pie at a gay teacher. A gay teacher who died of shame and embarrassment. Because silence equals death.

BLAKE: Let's remember the first Pride parade. Which may have begun as a lineup to buy the new Diana Ross album, but soon became a march into history.

CLAY: Let's remember the first lesbian rights organization, The Daughters of Bilitis. What became a ground-breaking call to arms began as a simple potluck.

BLAKE: Let's think about the brave people who fought for our rights during the riots at Stonehenge.

CLAY: I want a Pride I can feel proud of. That's why I've started slowing down and taking a more sober approach to the festivities.

BLAKE: So you're not taking the first Pride Weekend Keg Stand?

CLAY: Well, I can't break a thirty-year tradition.

BLAKE: And you've taken down the camera you installed in the locker room at GoodLife Fitness?*

CLAY: I would, but technically speaking Bell Media* owns it now.

BLAKE: And you're going to stop leading those Bait Bus tours?

CLAY: I just have such a rapport with the bait, you know?

BLAKE: It's true. Candy named you the godfather of her firstborn.

CLAY: That's what happens when you deliver a baby at the back of the Bait Bus.

BLAKE: It doesn't sound like you're slowing down at all.

CLAY: You're right. Maybe that's why I felt such a connection to that twink fresh off the bus from the methadone clinic. Because I, too, am taking it from both ends.

BLAKE: But no matter who you are, remember that Pride is a time to be proud.

CLAY: Proud of our history.

BLAKE: Proud of our future.

CLAY: So throw that first brick.

BLAKE: Host that damn potluck.

CLAY: And ask yourself: what would you say to eight-year-old…

BOTH: You?

Music plays as a NARRATOR announces the title:

TMI? NBD! Blake & Clay Q+A!

BLAKE: I've learned a lot tonight, Clay.

CLAY: So have I, Blake. And there is so much more to learn inside the pages of *Blake & Clay's Gay Agenda*.

BLAKE: On sale now in the bathroom at Glad Day.[4]

CLAY: We're working on getting it picked up by Frankie Grande's* new publishing house, The House of Publishing.

---

[4] Replace the bathroom at Glad Day with the bathroom of a well-known gay institution near you.

BLAKE: It's so great that he learned how to read.

CLAY: And what a great time to get into print media.

BLAKE: We had booked time for a Q+A with Dan Levy and Noah Reid.

CLAY: About something they both know a lot about:

BOTH: Gay rights.

BLAKE: But we're going to be brave and jump into it ourselves.

CLAY: I'm a little nervous. Talking about gay issues really should be left to the professionals.

BLAKE: Like Christine Baranski.

CLAY: Jennifer Coolidge.

BLAKE: Or the stars of Canadian sensation *Schitt's Creek*.

CLAY: But we'll do our best with the questions that were submitted by our lovely audience tonight.

BLAKE: Let's take a look.

                The NARRATOR reads the following questions, which may also appear as projections:

NARRATOR: As a baby gay, how can you begin to learn about the queer history that came before you?

BOTH: *Mommie Dearest.*

CLAY: Attending a screening of *Mommie Dearest* gives a young gay seventy-five percent of the cultural reference points he needs.

BLAKE:	The rest can be picked up by watching Liza Minnelli's appearances on the Home Shopping Network.
NARRATOR:	As an older gay, how do you get over fears of re-entering the nightlife scene?
BOTH:	Self-love.
CLAY:	I cannot stress how important it is to love yourself, no matter what age and weight you find yourself at.
BLAKE:	And I cannot stress how important it is to wear dark colours and vertical lines.
NARRATOR:	Did Olivia Colman really deserve the best actress Oscar for *The Favourite*?
BOTH:	Next question.
NARRATOR:	Should cops be allowed a float in the Pride parade?
BOTH:	No.
CLAY:	The police have yet to address their history of queer oppression and criminal negligence.
BLAKE:	They would better serve our community at this time by listening and learning.
NARRATOR:	I have a hard time in crowds, but I feel like I'm not doing enough for my community. Should I still be showing up to protests and demonstrations?

BLAKE & CLAY speak at the same time.

CLAY:	Yes	BLAKE:	No.

Pause.

> *The two grow more upset with one another as the questions continue, faster now.*

NARRATOR: I've lost touch with friends who recently chose a more traditional, monogamous lifestyle. Is it wrong to see their move as pro-establishment heteronormativity?

CLAY: No.   BLAKE: Yes.

NARRATOR: I'm not attracted to femme-presenting men. I think it's just a preference, but my friends say it's internalized homophobia. Am I being problematic?

CLAY: No.   BLAKE: Yes.

NARRATOR: My best friend told me that he's into piss play, and I was really uncomfortable. Was that kink-shaming?

CLAY: Yes.   BLAKE: No.

NARRATOR: My best friend is dating a man who shares an age and general facial structure with my friend's father. Am I right to be concerned?

CLAY: No.   BLAKE: Yes.

NARRATOR: All my friends are straight guys. I just get along with them better. Does that make me a bad gay?

CLAY: Yes.   BLAKE: No.

NARRATOR: I'm uncomfortable with straight women in gay bars. Does this make me a misogynist?

> *The two stop answering and begin to argue over one of the previous questions while the questions continue. This should be improvised.*

The audience should see this as a real argument, not one played for laughs.

The questions continue at rapid-fire, overlapping one another into cacophony.

NARRATOR: I recently discovered that an occasional hookup has started doing drag but thinking of them in women's clothing is a bit of a turnoff. Am I a bad person for not wanting to hook up again?

NARRATOR: I refuse to hook up with anyone above the age of thirty-eight, am I being ageist?

NARRATOR: I have a fetish for sleeping with men who are HIV+. Am I fetishizing a minority?

NARRATOR: If I have to listen to one more gay of a certain age try to teach me about the horrors of living through the AIDS crisis, I'm going to scream. Is it wrong to tell them I've heard it all before?

CLAY addresses the booth.

CLAY: Can we stop?

The questions stop. Silence.
Perhaps a long silence.

BLAKE addresses the audience.

CLAY: I still think about my first Pride parade. About how defiant it felt. And we were all so different, but there was still this little spark. This little something you could see in someone's eyes that said: *I know what it's like. I know you. I am you.* Last Pride I—

BLAKE's phone rings. He apologizes, but then shows the screen to CLAY. They chat quietly about whether to answer it. BLAKE answers on speakerphone.

Hello?

"DAN LEVY" speaks on the other end of the call.

DAN: Hi, Blake & Clay. It's me, Dan Levy.

BOTH: Dan Levy?!

DAN: That's right, boys.

BLAKE: Canada's very own!

DAN: Well, let's not go that far.

CLAY: We're so glad you got our email! You might have noticed that we attached our headshots for consideration in your next project.

DAN: Sorry, boys, but I just gave the parts of Elderly Gay Couple to Zachary Quinto and Andrew Rannells. They're on loan from the Ryan Murphy Collection.

CLAY: Oh, good choices.   BLAKE:
                                 They're very good.

BLAKE: Sorry if the vibes are a little off, Dan Levy.

CLAY: Blake and I were just having a bit of a tiff in front of our audience.

DAN: Well, boys, what seems to be the problem?

BLAKE: We can't agree on anything when it comes to gay politics.

CLAY: He says tomato, I say latex human urinal.

BLAKE: He says radical queer liberation, I say potato…and gravy and cheese curds and maybe some coleslaw.

CLAY: Sometimes it feels like we have more differences than similarities.

BLAKE:	Sometimes it feels like we're too busy digging in our heels to actually get anywhere.
CLAY:	Sometimes it feels like we're doing nothing but putting the cart before the horse.
BLAKE:	Sometimes I lie awake at night wondering if my father really loves me.
DAN:	Did you do an audience Q+A only to discover that you don't agree on every gay issue?
BOTH:	Yes, sir.
DAN:	Did you disagree about kink-shaming piss play?
BOTH:	Uh-huh.
DAN:	Now, boys, we're never going to agree on every aspect of the gay experience. Queer lives are unique and multifaceted. This should be celebrated while recognizing that our minor differences pale in comparison to the larger oppressions we all share. And piss play is gross. But that's what makes it so special.
BOTH:	Wow!
DAN:	Remember, boys. Gay life is a kaleidoscope of differing wants, needs, and choices. Fighting your fellow queer over minor differences does nothing but cede ground to a growing conservative fascism.
BOTH:	Really?
DAN:	They're coming for our rights, boys! And they're hoping we're too busy fighting each other to fight back.

CLAY: That really puts things into perspective.

BLAKE: I'm glad you called, Dan Levy. We really needed to hear that.

DAN: I actually called to let you know that I didn't agree for my name or likeness to be used in this presentation, and that you'll be hearing from my lawyers with a cease and de—

                 BLAKE hangs up with a beep.

BLAKE: Well, folks, I hope you learned a lot today! I know we sure did. I learned to let go of my sexual shame. Because there will always be someone there to shame me for having that shame.

CLAY: I learned that there is still violence and bigotry towards queer families, but to never discount the power of queer resilience. The only thing to discount are Tide PODS®.

BLAKE: I learned that when it comes to mental health, self-care is so important.

CLAY: Which is why I said *no* when Derek asked if he could stop by my apartment to pick up his insulin.

BLAKE: That's huge.

CLAY: It's important to set boundaries.

BLAKE: I learned that honest depictions of queer characters can only come from writing your truth. And the truths of a focus group of twelve angry pansexuals with asymmetrical haircuts.

CLAY: We learned that our differences are what make us strong.

BLAKE: That queer perfectionism is as puritanical as conservatism.

CLAY: But mostly we learned that *Blake & Clay's Gay Agenda* is only $24.99.

BLAKE: And on sale now at the Church and Wellesley Pizza Pizza.[5]

CLAY: Thanks for coming, everyone, but we've gotta go!

BLAKE: There's another show coming in—

CLAY: About a young man's journey of self-discovery on one fateful day in Gander, Newfoundland.

BLAKE: It's called *Come From A Gay*.

CLAY: Written by a young man named Dillon.

BOTH: He has a BA in musical theatre! Good night!

BLAKE & CLAY leave, chatting excitedly about how well their book launch went.

End of play.

---

[5] Replace "Church and Wellesley Pizza Pizza" with a local pizza place or a fast food joint in your gay neighbourhood.